Walks & Rambles in

WESTCHESTER AND FAIRFIELD COUNTIES

Walks & Rambles in
WESTCHESTER
AND FAIRFIELD
COUNTIES

A Nature Lover's Guide to 30 Parks & Sanctuaries

KATHERINE S. ANDERSON

Backcountry Publications
Woodstock, Vermont

An Invitation to the Reader

If you find that conditions have changed along these walks, please let the author and publisher know so that corrections may be made in future printings. If you wish to be advised of significant trail relocations, or other changes affecting the walking routes mentioned in this guide, send us your name, address, and the title of this book. Address all correspondence to:

Editor
Walks and Rambles Series
Backcountry Publications
P.O. Box 175
Woodstock, VT 05091

Library of Congress Cataloging-in-Publication Data

Anderson, Katherine S., 1926-
  Walks and rambles in Westchester and Fairfield
Countries.

  1. Walking — New York (State) — Westchester County —
Guide-books. 2. Walking — Connecticut — Fairfield
County — Guide-books. 3. Natural history — New York
(State) — Westchester County. 4. Natural history —
Connecticut — Fairfield County. 5. Westchester
County (N.Y.) — Description and travel. 6. Fairfield
County (Conn.) — Description and travel. I. Title.
GV199.42.N42W442 1986   917.47'277   85-28570
ISBN 0-942440-29-3 (pbk.)

Published by Backcountry Publications, Inc.
Woodstock, Vermont 05091
Printed in the United States of America

Design by Ann Aspell
Maps and calligraphy by Alex Wallach
Photographs by the author
Line drawings by Pamela Anderson

Twenty-four of these walks were originally published in *The North County News*, Yorktown, New York. They are printed here in revised form, with permission.

Contents

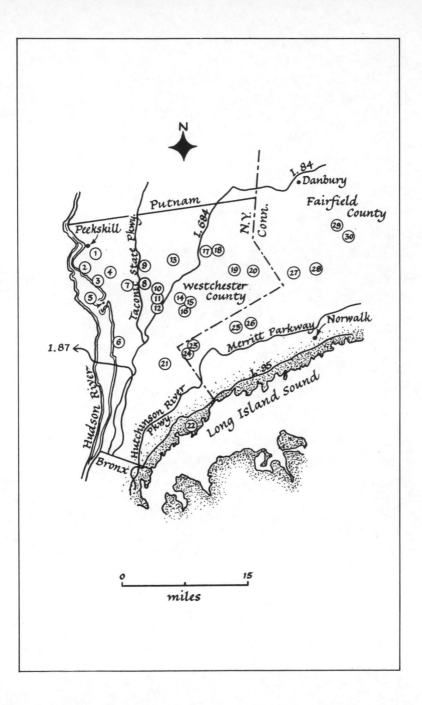

Introduction

DESPITE THE RAPID GROWTH OF HOUSING, shopping malls, and corporate world headquarters, Westchester and Fairfield Counties have within their borders many areas that retain the flavor of the wilderness that once was here. Thirty of these places have been gathered in this book. This is not a book of hikes, but a book of gentle walks (which is not to say that there are no hills to climb or rocks to scramble over). They are offered with the hope that they will refresh your spirit as they increase your knowledge of the natural world.

Sizes of the properties vary from six acres to almost five thousand. Larger places, such as Ward Pound Ridge Reservation and Devil's Den, have many other trails besides those covered here. You can obtain complete area maps when you visit them. Whether called park, preserve, sanctuary, or reservation, the lands described herein are considered to be protected against exploitation of any plant or animal. There is much here for you to enjoy because the people who came before you have left the wilderness virtually intact.

Most of the places in this book are open from dawn to dusk. Usually trails are open even on days when nature centers are closed. A few areas, primarily the Westchester County parks, charge nominal parking fees. Camping is available at only two of the parks, Croton Point and Ward Pound Ridge Reservation. The walks in this book are organized in a west-to-east sequence, starting at the Hudson River and ending in Fairfield County, Connecticut.

Where walks are close together, you may like to take more than one. For example, Graff Sanctuary and Croton Point, both in Croton, would make a nice combination. In Chappaqua, Pinecliff Sanctuary and Choate Sanctuary or Gedney Brook Sanctuary could be visited in one day. In Redding, a longer walk at Huntington State Park might be followed by a shorter walk and a picnic at Putnam Memorial Park.

Many of the organizations that maintain these sanctuaries are composed primarily of volunteers. For that reason you will not find

1

trails in pristine condition at all times. You might like to add a small pair of clippers to your backpack and give a hand to some of these workers. Even in county and state parks, maintenance is very often the last item in the budget. In addition, nature itself is always making changes, such as the elimination of a particular wildflower by replacement with other species or the downing of trees in storms.

Most trail markings are on trees. Paint is considerably harder to vandalize than plastic or metal markers. Marks vary. The Appalachian Trail system (three dots indicating the beginning or end of a trail, two indicating a turn coming up) is used by many. In others, including Pierrepont State Park, simple white bands are painted around the trees. See the legend at the end of this introduction for other map information.

You know how you like to dress for walking. Nevertheless, it is important to mention the need for adequate footgear. Concealed slippery roots, rolling rocks, or inadequately cut spikes of saplings can cause trouble. (For this reason it is advisable to carry an ace bandage in your pack.) Some people like to hike in shorts in warm weather. Long pants, however, will protect you much more from mosquito bites, ticks, and the all-pervasive poison ivy. From shad flies in early spring to deer flies in summer and mosquitos almost any time, some kind of nuisance insect is almost always with us. Many people like to use repellants, and some find hats are helpful. You will soon discover what works best for you.

As far as equipment is concerned, your own interests will dictate. A hand lens will add immeasurably to your pleasure. Binoculars can be used for distant botanizing as well as for watching birds. Field guides are always helpful, especially if your companions carry different ones from yours.

My friends and I have a saying, "Never leave home without your lunch." Certainly a high-energy snack is a good idea, and water, especially during hot weather. Be sure someone knows where you are going and when you expect to return, most important if you like to walk alone.

I have tried to discuss something of particular interest at each location. However, since many of these woodlands are similar, you will meet old friends in every one. Where registry boxes exist, it is helpful to the property managers if you enter your name. You might also note any interesting sightings that other people would like to share. Because the laws of the State of New York, especially, require these lands to be used for educational purposes, it is important for their managers to know how many people are taking advantage of their availability.

My thanks to many friends who have helped me explore these walks. Also to my three children, without whom the book would never have been written. And special thanks to my editor, Susan Edwards, from whom I learned so much during our months of work together.

"...they do not die poorest who have helped to add one gleam of healthy pleasure to the lives of their fellow creatures, or increased by one tiny grain the sum total of human knowledge."

Richard Kearton, 1902, from the introduction to the sixth edition of Gilbert White's *Natural History of Selbourne*.

MAP LEGEND

parking area	Ⓟ
main trail	● ● ● ●
side trail or alternate route	· · · ·
point of interest	X
fields	⬭
marsh	ⱴⱴ ⱴⱴ
building	■
bridge	⌒
cemetery	†
boardwalk	● ● ● ●
trail boundary	● ● ●│● ● ●
boulder	▲
point of elevation	▲
corduroy bridge/logs	●│││││││●
stone wall	〰〰〰

WESTCHESTER COUNTY

Brinton Brook Sanctuary

1. Blue Mountain Reservation

Location: Peekskill, New York
Distance: 3 miles
Access: From NY 9 exit at Welcher Avenue. Follow Welcher east all the way to its end at the reservation entrance. A minimal parking fee is charged during the summer.
Owner: County of Westchester

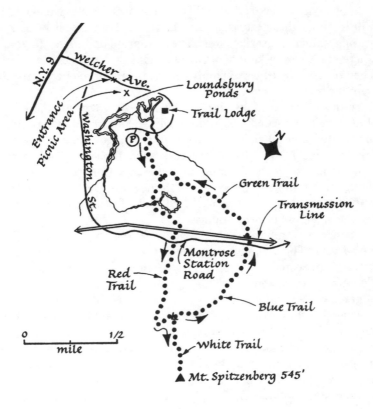

HERE IS ONE OF THE PLACES IN WESTCHESTER County where stimulating walks will reward you with magnificent views. In the Blue Mountain Reservation, the prospect from Mount Spitzenberg is one of the best.

Blue Mountain is a multiple-use park. It offers a sportsmen's center for fishing, archery, and rifle practice, a bathing lake, and a picnic area. A fine trail lodge can be rented for conferences. But the park's biggest asset is its natural beauty.

Park your car in the lot past the trail lodge. There are usually Canada geese on the lawn next to Loundsbury Pond. As recently as the 1960s these geese would have been a rare sight in the county except during migration. Now they have become a "nuisance bird" because of their increasing numbers.

In order to understand why this has happened you have to know a little about the lifestyle of Canada geese. These regal birds are grazing animals, just like cows. They eat grass and prefer to graze where the grass is kept short. Lawns and golf courses are ideal. They nest on the edges of ponds which, before developers arrived, were marshes and swamps.

Because their goslings take a long time to grow up, the geese tend to be fairly sedentary. Additionally, in late June and early July the adults molt all their primary feathers at one time. Since the geese cannot fly for a couple of weeks while their new feathers are growing in, they must be near water to escape from predators. The timing of this molt and the growth of the new wing feathers coincides with the growth of the goslings' first flight feathers, so the whole family becomes airborne at once.

Geese are faithful mates and a goose family stays together for a whole year. The young of this summer will be chased away when nesting time comes next spring. Geese must be three or four years old before they can breed, which explains the occasional small flocks of geese without young.

Several solutions to the Canada geese problem have been suggested, but the only one that will work is to let the grass grow tall — not very practical for golf courses. Trapping and removing the geese works only until they can fly again, when back they come. They are game birds and delicious eating, but very few are shot in Westchester (hunting laws apply). You just have to admire their beauty, their courage, their family loyalty, and remember that their droppings are processed grass which makes good fertilizer.

Leave the geese behind, and start up the Red Trail, which begins opposite the lodge. Blue Mountain Reservation is noted for its magnificent rock formations, and this trail takes you through or around many of them. Look for little natural rock gardens of grasses, ferns, and even natural bonsai trees in crevices. Mosses and lichens are abundant.

Water is also abundant in the park. The trail passes one small woodland pond which is usually well populated by frogs and salamanders. This pond also has many clumps of tussock sedge with its feet in the water, last year's brown leaves hanging down like hair, and new bright green growth at the top. If you feel the stem of a sedge you will find it is triangular. The stems of reeds are round, and those of grasses are round with joints.

Two shrubs predominate along the trail. One is the maple-leaved viburnum, whose name describes the shape of its leaves but not

Sailing vessels such as the sloop Clearwater can often be seen from the top of Mt. Spitzenberg.

their velvety softness. In June it has small clusters of tiny creamy flowers in flat heads, which will be followed by dark blue berries. At flowering time it may be possible to see feeding the tiny pink-green-and-white caterpillar of the spring azure butterfly. These caterpillars are often attended by small ants, which like to eat the honeydew that the caterpillar exudes.

The other shrub is one of our most spectacular native Americans, the mountain laurel. Its buds, looking like decorations for a fancy cake, and its wide-open flowers have a unique beauty. Many flowers are specialized in some way to encourage pollination by insects. The laurel flower has stamens caught at their tips in depressions in each petal. When a bee lands on a flower cup to reach for the sweet nectar in its center, the insect's weight releases these stamens and pollen is sprinkled on the bee's back. The pollen is thereby carried on to another flower, and thus seed production begins. You can use your finger as the "bee weight" to see this happen. Laurel is evergreen; the thick stands that occur in our woodlands provide good winter cover for birds and deer.

There are several riding stables in the vicinity of Blue Mountain, and the use of its trails by horses is evident. Along the Red Trail you will cross two open spaces. One is a pipeline; the other is Montrose Station Road, a dirt road which traverses the park. Both of these openings provide a different habitat for animals and an "edge." An edge occurs where two habitats, such as woodland and field, meet. It is always the most heavily populated part of any area.

Where the Red Trail intersects the Blue, turn left for a short distance and look for the White Trail on your right. This will take you, after a short steep climb of about 100 feet, to the top of Mount Spitzenberg.

What a view rewards the climb! The Hudson River with the upper Palisades on its west side, the Tappan Zee Bridge, and Hook Mountain, where hawks sail by in the fall. The F.D.R. Veterans' Hospital is below, along with a large apartment complex which looks like a freight train wreck. Imagine this view during the days of the Revolution, when all this land had been cleared. You really could have sat up here with a spy glass and watched the activities of British armies some distance away.

There are many options for the return trip. A nice way to go is back to the Blue Trail, turn right, then bear left on the Green Trail after crossing Montrose Station Road. All trails are clearly marked.

10

2. George's Island

Location: Montrose, New York

Distance: 1 mile

Access: From Route 9, exit at Montrose. Go north on 9A for 1.3 miles. Turn left onto Dutch Street (at a large sign for George's Island). The entrance is at the end of the street. A minimal parking fee is charged on weekends and in the summer.

Owner: County of Westchester

GEORGE'S ISLAND IS A PENINSULA EXTENDING
into the Hudson River. Natural areas, picnic areas, and river views
each contribute to the park's appeal.

Leave your car in the first parking lot, to the left of the toll booth.
A labeled nature trail begins at the lot's south corner. This trail was
built by the Youth Conservation Corps in 1980. A self-guiding pam-
phlet is available from the park's manager.

As is true in all old estate areas of this region, many non-native
plants are mixed in here with naturally occuring ones. Multiflora
rose and honeysuckle are two. A large white pine has dropped its
cones to the path. These cones have scales which are very sensitive
to dampness. By closing up when wet, white pine scales protect
the winged seeds between them. On dry breezy days when the
cones open, the seeds are released. They fly to new patches of
ground, where they have a better chance of sprouting than they
would have had under the parent tree.

Bear right at an intersection with another trail. Here is your first
glimpse of the river. On the right of the trail, near a large rock, is
a hop hornbeam tree. This tree is usually found farther north. In
the fall its seeds hang in clusters, each enclosed in a brown papery
capsule. At the overlook, growing among the rocks, are some large
chestnut oaks. These oaks, with their strongly furrowed bark, prefer
to grow on rocky hilltops. The "chestnut" in their name refers to
their leaves, which look like those of chestnut trees. Rock oak might
be a better name.

The trail goes down the hill to the right. Bear left at a "Y" junction
to go down to the river. In April look for Dutchman's-breeches and
columbine among the rocks on the left of the path. This trail dead-
ends at the river. Walk back up to the base of the hill, and then
bear right to walk up onto the ball field near the parking area.
Along the way you can compare the leaves or the leaf scars, depend-
ing on season, of staghorn sumac and ailanthus. The leaf scars of
ailanthus are very large horseshoes, while those of sumac completely
surround the bud.

Cross the field to the road, and turn left, back toward the river.
There are beautiful willows along the way. One is the weeping
willow, with long pendant branches. The other is the black willow,
with more upright branches. Swans nest on a small pond to your
right, and longbilled marsh wrens sing from phragmites, tall reeds
which grow in wet areas.

12

Smashing waves and grinding ice have helped to shape the dramatic rocks of the Hudson shore.

Take the right at the end of the pond. This trail is very overgrown along the edges, an almost impenetrable thicket that is wonderful cover for birds and rabbits. Cottontail rabbits do not dig burrows in the ground but rest in small depressions called forms under thick shrubs. They are not rodents, because their incisors are different; however they use their incisors as rodents do to cut their plant food. Rabbits are prolific breeders. The nest is a shallow hole in the ground, covered with a blanket of dry grass and fur from the female's body when she is not in attendance. The female, called a doe, visits the nest at dawn and dusk to feed her young. At the age of six weeks these little bunnies are own their own, and the doe proceeds to bear another litter. Very few of the little ones survive their first hazardous summer of life.

Beyond the thicket the trail leads to a knoll which overlooks a large pond. In the early 20th century the Hudson valley was known for its brick industry. Many buildings in New York City, as well as in Westchester, were built from bricks made at George's Island. This pond was a clay pit and is reputed to be 80 feet deep. It is fresh water and is not connected to the river. The local name for the pond is Lake Whoopee; you will see evidence of such activities around its edge. On the far side is an extensive growth of narrow-leaved cattail, where birds such as Virginia rails like to hide. You can see the clay for which this area was famous in the trail itself. If the path is wet it can be slippery.

Return along the same trail. Look for thimbleweed blooming in

13

June. This white flower will be followed by a cluster of seeds, tightly wound up with soft fibers and shaped like a thimble.

Back on the road, cross the lower parking lot and bear right toward the picnic shelter. If you look up into the shelter's roof you will see two kinds of nests made of mud. One is the nest of the barn swallow, a dark blue-and-orange bird with a forked tail which feeds on flying insects. Because it builds in sheltered places like this, a barn swallow may use the same nest year after year. Most other birds make new nests each spring.

The other mud nest is made by a mud dauber wasp and is actually a brood chamber for its young. When a mud tube or clump is complete, the female wasp provisions it with paralyzed spiders, then adds newly laid eggs and seals the chamber. The eggs hatch into larvae which feed on the spiders. They go through the pupal stage within the chambers and emerge as adult wasps in the spring. Many of these wasps are electric blue in color, and may be seen collecting building material around the edges of mud puddles. They are docile, and there is no need to fear them.

Bear to the right along a path that runs on a bank above the water's edge. The Stony Point monument is visible across the river. Look out over the cove for feeding ducks. In winter loons may be seen here. The common loon, which nests on northern lakes, spends the winter along the coast or in rivers like this, calmly feeding in waters so cold we could not survive in them. Loons are very ancient birds. Their fossilized remains have been found in rocks 67 million years old. The name "loon" comes from a Scandanavian word meaning clumsy. The bird's legs are set so far back on its body it cannot walk on land. These legs mean that loons are accomplished swimmers. They are known to dive as deep as 240 feet below the surface and stay under for as long as three minutes.

Walking along this path, you will see signs of former human occupation. The early Indians left most of the oyster shells. During the 1920s a mansion still existed here, with cabins, a tennis court, and a ball field. One of the major users of the site was the American Canoe Association. Flotillas of canoes used to paddle from Dyckman Street in Manhattan to this peninsula for outings. Westchester County purchased the land from the federal government in 1959.

Interesting plants along this path include hackberry trees, seaside goldenrod, and a very large swamp white oak. The path circles the point and returns to the parking lot.

3. Graff Sanctuary

Location: Croton, New York

Distance: 1.25 miles

Access: From NY 9A going north, turn left onto Furnace Dock
Road just before the entrance to a Daitch Shopwell super-
market. After about 0.25 mile, look for the sanctuary's entrance near the third telephone pole after a brown house on
the left. The sign is set high. Roadside parking.

Owner: National Audubon Society
(Managed by Saw Mill River Audubon Society)

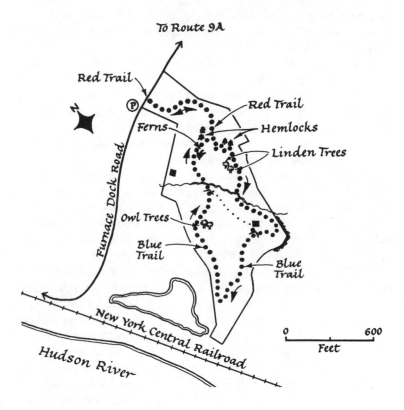

ITS PROXIMITY TO AND VIEWS OF THE HUDSON River give Graff Sanctuary a special flavor. The sanctuary is also unusual in that a large part of its forest consists of magnificent tall tulip trees mixed with large Norway maples. The introduced maples, along with such shrubs as molle viburnum, come from the days when there were several large landscaped estates in the area. On the other side of Furnace Dock Road is a county park, Oscawana. As yet undeveloped, it is nice to wander in.

At the Graff Sanctuary entrance three red dots on a rock in the wall indicate the start of the Red Trail, which leads steeply down to a damp area. In winter, if there is ice underfoot, walking there may be difficult. Turn left at the first intersection. From the valley floor, with its spice bush and springtime jack-in-the-pulpit, the trail goes in switchbacks up through hemlocks. Some of the chestnut oaks near the top of this hostile rocky hillside have died, and their bark is falling off in thick chunks. Mycelia of honey mushrooms cling to the exposed wood.

We are high above the valley now, with nice views back. In late summer the open deciduous woods at the top have a thick ground cover of white woodland asters, each plant a delicate bouquet. Later, their empty seed receptacles will shine in the winter sun. As we start down the hill on the other side (not so steep), we will pass a linden, or basswood, tree with seven trunks of similar size, all apparently coming from one root system. This tree produces white wood valued for carving. The Indians made rope from its tough fibrous bark, which is so strong it cannot be broken by hand.

Crossing the brook below depends a little on the water's depth — you may have to look around for a series of good stepping stones. Still some trail maintenance to be done here! In spring the brook flows through a carpet of trout lilies.

The Red Trail bears to the left and follows along the ridge above the brook to a stone wall, thence curving around to the right again. Continue on as you sight a large stone building. This peculiar structure with stone steps to lure you to its top was apparently part of a water system for the estate on the Oscawana property. At one time there was a hole in its top, but that has been cemented over for safety's sake. No other holes are apparent, nor are pipes. Whatever its original purpose, the structure now provides a wonderful place to sit among the treetops and watch for birds and other animals.

Go back on the Red Trail a bit, and take the Blue Trail on your right. It wanders through a small forest consisting primarily of black locust trees, which attest to the young age of this part of the woods. Black locust is one of the "pioneer" trees, among the first to colonize old fields. There is also a tangle of honeysuckle vines underfoot, something of a nuisance to walk through. Honeysuckle's only redeeming feature is that deer and rabbits like to eat it. If only they would eat it faster!

On your left, a line of old fence posts parallels the Blue Trail for awhile, a further remnant of the farming era. We are heading toward the river now; you can see it glistening through the trees and feel the wind sharpen. The sound of an occasional train reminds us that we are not far from civilization. On windy winter days you may hear ice grinding along the Hudson's eastern shore. You cannot actually get to the river from here because of the terrain's steepness, but the views are nice. At this point you also overlook a small lake (on private property) frequented by kingfishers and ospreys. Since the lake is less turbulent and murky than the river, it is an easier place for these birds to fish.

The Blue Trail bends away from the river and follows along the edge of a steep descent to a gorge. Hemlocks cast deep shadows. If you look carefully as the trail bends to the right and starts up a small hill, you will find evidence of the great horned owls that live in this sanctuary. "Whitewash" can be seen on some of the tree trunks, and remains of owl pellets can be found on the ground. These pellets are made of hair and bone from the owls' food. They are cast from the birds' mouths and are not unpleasant to handle if they are dry. In them you can find recognizable skulls, claws, and various bones. The large rabbit population in this sanctuary is doubtless one of its attractions for owls, because rabbits are the preferred food of these fierce tigers of the air. If the crows are active they may show you where one of the owls is roosting. Since crows are also on the owls' menu, they will harrass any owl they find sleeping in the daytime.

Follow the Blue Trail back to its intersection with the Red, and bear left. You will pass beautiful rock formations and several steep-sided small gorges. The Red Trail bears right near some more old fence posts. The trail passes through a thick bed of Christmas ferns. On the right is a rock shoulder covered with polypody ferns and

17

partridge berry. Ferns have a long and complicated life cycle. Rarely do we see "baby" ferns, for they are so small they are hard to observe. Spores released from the dots on the backs of fern leaves grow into minute plants called gametophytes. Sexual parts develop within each gametophyte. When the egg and sperm unite, usually through transportation of sperm in water, a sporophyte develops. Conditions must be perfect for a sporophyte to become a mature fern; most of the billions of spores produced never complete the cycle.

The Red Trail bears left just past a small hemlock grove, and retraces the first part of the walk back to the sanctuary entrance. If you would like to go down to the river, drive down Furnace Dock Road. It will bring you to a parking area where there used to be a train station. The bridge over the tracks here is not safe. Continue on around the curve, and you will come to a pull-off area on your left, with a trail going out to a nice rocky shore along the river. (This is county property.) Continuing on this road will bring you to Crugers Station Road and back to 9A, or you can retrace your route.

4. Brinton Brook Sanctuary

Location: Croton, New York

Distance: 1.5 miles

Access: From NY 9 exit at Senasqua Road. Go left (north) on
  NY 9A (Old Albany Post Road). After passing Sky View
  nursing home, continue 0.3 mile. Look for a sign on the
  right: "Kenoten, Weinstein, Private Drive." Turn right here
  and follow the drive about 0.5 mile to the sanctuary parking lot.

Owner: National Audubon Society

  (Managed by Saw Mill River Audubon Society)

WILLARD AND LAURA BRINTON FOUND THEIR
homesite by walking from Peekskill and following a topographic
map. When Laura Brinton donated this land to National Audubon
in 1957, she called it a "living museum of this region." If you are
interested in birds, plants, geology, or water, there is something
here for you to enjoy.

From the parking lot, take the Yellow Trail to the south (through
the fence to the right, not straight ahead). This trail runs along the
base of a hill. It is a wonderful sun trap in winter. The snarls of
grapevines among the trees provide excellent cover and food for
small birds and ruffed grouse. You can expect to "put up" at least
one of the latter in this area. Apparently the grouse can control the
amount of noise it makes on takeoff. Sometimes it rises with a
thunderous sound which is really startling, and sometimes it rises
in complete silence. There is a theory that some of the loud noises
animals make, such as the slapping of beavers' tails or the takeoff
of grouse, are not just for warning but are intended to throw predators off balance by startling them, making the predators reveal
their locations. It does seem to me, though, that grouse tend to be
quieter during the hunting season.

Lots of deer sign can be found in this area, too. Deer are browsers,
and a close look at the twigs of shrub dogwoods or low-growing

19

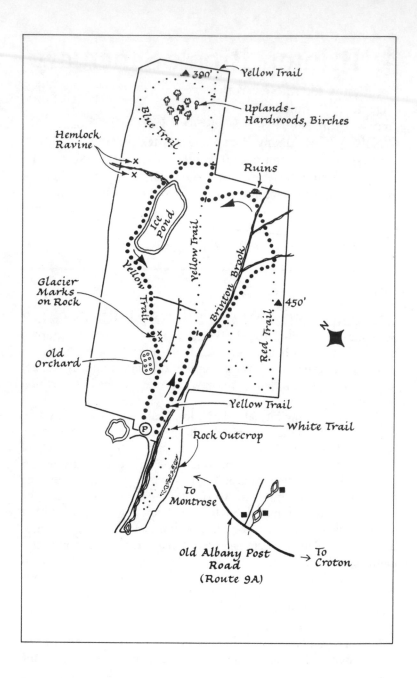

▲ 390' — Yellow Trail

Uplands – Hardwoods, Birches

Blue Trail

Hemlock Ravine

Ruins

Ice Pond

Yellow Trail

Brinton Brook

Glacier Marks on Rock

Yellow Trail

▲ 450'

Red Trail

Old Orchard

Yellow Trail

White Trail

P

Rock Outcrop

N

To Montrose

Old Albany Post Road
(Route 9A)

To Croton

maples reveal shredded ends. Deer have no teeth in the front of their upper jaws; they twist and pull twigs with their lower jaw teeth working against a hard pad in the upper jaw. One deer is said to consume between 15 and 20 pounds of this material each day. They are ruminants, like cows. They can browse as they walk along, then lie up somewhere in hiding, regurgitate the material and chew it, swallowing it down again for complete digestion.

Turn right on the Red Trail. Ahead is a thick, dark hemlock forest. The brook crossing is a good place to see raccoon tracks. In the center of the hemlock grove stands a giant tree, probably 200 years old, the parent of all the other hemlocks here. Look for owl pellets beneath it. This trail leads us to one of Brinton's most appealing features, the split rock spring. A stone seat invites you to sit a while near water bubbling from the split in a huge rock. The water temperature in the pools (which were built by Mr. Brinton, an engineer and inventor) stays almost the same year-round — 48 degrees. As a result the pools rarely freeze, and tadpoles and frogs can sometimes be seen even in winter. In early spring egg masses of spotted salamanders are attached to twigs below the water's surface.

Continue on the Red Trail, crossing a small dam. At the next intersection turn left, still on the Red Trail. This section takes you along another hillside and past some old foundations. The story of the foundations, as told to me by Mrs. Brinton, is that a slave named Jesse Davis ran away from his masters before the Civil War and went to sea as a pirate ship cook. When the war was over and black people emancipated, Jesse took his earnings and built a little subsistence farm at this spot. We don't know how long he lived here, or which of these foundations was house and which barn. Probably it was Jesse who kept this land cleared for many years. The stream that we just crossed would have been his water supply.

Eventually the Red Trail meets the Yellow Trail again. Turn right on the Yellow. This trail is an old farm road, somewhat depressed, with stone walls along each side. It can be very wet in spring. Make a left on the Yellow Trail where it meets the Blue Trail. You will pass another intersection with the Blue Trail. Now slowly and quietly approach the ice pond. Great blue herons, green herons, and various ducks may be surprised here. The trail goes across the stone and earth dam which retains the pond. Five acres in extent, the pond was built as a source of ice. Unfortunately for the entrepreneur who built it, shortly after the pond filled someone invented the electric refrigerator, and his ice business soon disappeared.

The pond contains green frogs, bull frogs, many varieties of fish, and some of the biggest snapping turtles alive. One, seen here sunning on a rock, had a tail as thick as your wrist. Snapping turtles prey on ducklings as well as fish. Big turtles have no natural enemies; their populations are mainly kept in check by raccoons and skunks, who eat turtle eggs. Turtle nests are dug in sunny spots. Sometimes you find twisted pieces of leathery shell near a small hole, evidence of a midnight feast.

The trail continues through several open fields, which are mowed each October with a tractor in order to keep them from reverting to forest. Summer is their most beautiful time, with clumps of orange butterfly weed, yellow black-eyed Susans, white yarrow, and a beautiful grass called Indian grass — all in bloom. An annual butterfly count here in July by Saw Mill River Audubon has recorded as many as nineteen different species.

Past the meadows, on the left, is a huge rock shoulder of gneiss, smoothed and grooved by glacial action ten thousand years ago. This is a great place to climb up and sit quietly for awhile, observing what's going on in the trees and thickets across the path. In spring and summer you should hear, and I hope you will see, an indigo bunting, one of the most beautiful of blue birds. Blue feathers do not have blue pigment. The color is structural, caused by the reflection or refraction of light rays — the feathers are actually gray. Find a blue jay feather; hold it up to the light and look through it. You will see that it is gray. Yet the three blue birds of our area — blue jay, indigo bunting, and bluebird — look brilliantly blue.

The trail passes through an old apple orchard, another remnant of farming days. The trees are slowly dying and falling, but those left still produce fruit. There is a pear tree, too. In the fall this is a good place to see deer and box turtles feeding on fallen fruits. It is a good place for birds year-round. The registry book is kept here in the orchard, in a drawer, along with a map of the sanctuary. Vandalism has made the Audubon naturalists who work here move the book out of the parking area. From this point the trail goes directly back to your car.

22

5. Croton Point Park

Location: Croton, New York

Distance: 2 miles

Access: From NY 9 exit at Croton/Harmon. Turn west toward the railroad station. A light regulates traffic over a very narrow bridge. Go past the dump to the large parking lot. A minimal fee is charged from Memorial Day to Labor Day.

Owner: County of Westchester

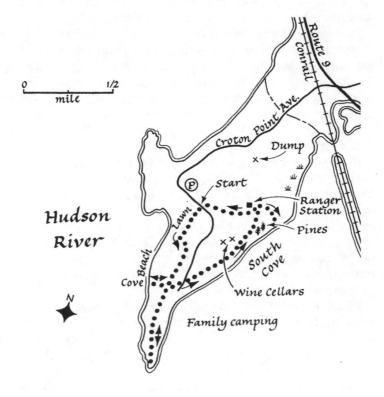

CROTON POINT IS ONE OF THE MOST BEAUTIFUL
parks in Westchester. A visit to it provides a grand overview of the
way we have desecrated much of our land, and yet saved some of
the best. If this sounds contradictory, just come out and take a look.
Bur first check the tide tables in the daily paper; low tide is the
time to go.

With gigantic garbage trucks on their way to or coming from the
famous Croton landfill, you must wait your turn to cross the narrow
bridge. The landfill has been one of the most controversial county
activities in recent years. Twenty years ago it was indeed a "filling"
action; but with the passage of time, and increase in population
and the amount of rubbish, we now have a mountain of garbage.
Despite strict regulations on the amount of dirt cover to be added
daily, the odor of this mountain can be overwhelming.

Plans are set for the closing of this dump. Its ultimate fate is not
settled, but the land probably will become part of the park. What
will happen to the thousands of birds dependent on this garbage
for their food — the gulls of several varieties, the crows, the star-
lings? Nowhere would there seem to be left enough natural habitat
to support so many. Probably their health will improve as their
numbers go down. It is not unusual to see a gull stricken with
poisoning from something it ate.

From your parked car, walk westward to the magnificent Hudson
River. On most good days you will see fishermen along the shore.
The Hudson, though it has suffered mightily at the hands of man,
is now making a comeback. Fish and other animals, such as shad
and blue crabs, are increasing. Of course it is not safe to eat all of
them because of chemical residues including PCBs in their bodies,
but at least they can live in the river now. It is hoped that in the
future more chemicals will be eliminated, as fewer go into the river
from industrial sources.

Much of the lawn area on which we are standing is fill. It was
made in the same way as the dump behind us. Along the beach
farther to the south, winter storms often tear off great chunks of
soil, exposing bottles, plastic bags — old garbage that has been
used to support new land.

There are several very special reasons for visiting Croton Point.
One of the best is beachcombing — the reason to go at low tide.
As you walk along the grassy picnic area (a great place for kite
flying) you will approach the beach. Treasures can be found here.

24

The driftwood alone would be hard to resist, if it were not lying so far from the car. There may be huge trees, some with roots still intact, polished to a silver sheen by the water's action. There are tiny pieces of driftwood in animal shapes. Then there is the residue of past ages: broken bits of brick, also polished by the water, remnants of the Point's old brick-making industry; shards of china; polished colored glass; a teaspoon from a doll's tea set. You may find skeletons of fish, left by fishermen or washed up dead and scavenged by the gulls.

Two favorite things to search for are caltrops and clay babies. Caltrops are seeds from the water chestnut, a plant that grows under water. They are black and hard, with four points positioned in such a way that no matter how they rest on the ground, one point sticks up. During the Middle Ages, when war was fought on horseback, metal caltrops were made and flung on the field of battle in the hope that enemy horses would step on them and become disabled. Imagine stepping on one of these in your bare feet! Though the seeds originally within these containers are supposed to be edible, they are almost impossible to find. The submerged stems of the water chestnut are a hazard to navigation, as they can foul ship propellors.

Clay babies are unique formations made when water seeps through the banks of clay that line Croton Point (clay from which bricks were once made). When the water meets an obstruction (such as a grain of sand), lime, precipitated out, forms weird shapes. Geologists call these "concretions." They are light gray in color, and they feel chalky when they are rubbed. The first one is hard to find, but after you know what clay babies look like — and they look like everything from animals to small humans — they seem to pop out at you from the thousands of stones on the beach.

If the tide is low enough, you can walk along the beach to a small cove where a short steep trail leads to the top of the bank. Otherwise, retrace your steps along the beach, and look for a trail going into the woods on your right where the lawn begins. Up this trail you will arrive at the camp area. During the summer the cabins here can be rented, and it is apt to be rather crowded, but from September until June you can enjoy solitary walking on land that has a long and interesting history. Indians of the Kitchawan tribe used the Point as a spring fishing place, and there are oyster middens (heaps of discarded shells) all along the shore. Some of these shells are thousands of years old. Oysters no longer grow in the Hudson, probably not because of pollution but because of altered siltation and salinity changes — oysters are very sensitive to both.

After the Indians, Van Cortlands owned this land. Perhaps the most interesting later owners were the Underhill brothers, who hybridized native grapes with European strains. Prior to that time (early 1800s) European grapes had not grown well in this country because they could not withstand local insects and diseases. Underhill wines were reputed to be of great medicinal value and were highly recommended by doctors. The magnificent English yew trees midway out on the point were planted by the Underhills, whose house stood in that area.

Out at Croton Point's tip, you have a beautiful view of the widest place in the Hudson, the Tappan Zee, spanned by the graceful bridge of that name. The high promontory on the right is Hook Mountain, an excellent place for hawk watching on fall days (Croton Point is good, too). Rock formations along the western shore of the river are part of the Palisades.

As you are walking back from the Point, take a dirt road downhill to the right. Feel the sun pouring into this southern exposure! This is an excellent place to see birds at any season. The dump, of course, provides raptors with many a tasty rat, and owls and hawks are commonly seen on the Point. Near the bottom of the slope, on the left, are two old Underhill wine cellars built into the side of the hill.

Past the pine grove, take a turn to the right. This will bring you down to the edge of South Cove. Across the cove is Sing Sing prison. The muddy edges of tide pools here are good places to look for tracks of raccoon, opossum, and muskrat. Ducks float on the cove.

You will have to retrace your steps from the edge of the cove back to the pine forest. Then go straight up the hill past the ranger's house. Take another long look at this dump. If you have the feeling you throw away too much — good. You probably do. Recycle! The Indian middens are actually garbage dumps several thousands of years old. But modern man is leaving too much for the archeologists of the year 5000 to do.

6. Rockefeller State Park Preserve

Location: Pocantico Hills, New York

Distance: 1.5 miles

Access: From NY 9A or the Taconic State Parkway, take the exit for NY 117. Drive west 0.3 mile to a light. Turn left on NY 448. At 0.1 mile, turn right on Old Sleepy Hollow Road. Continue 1.6 miles to the intersection with Sleepy Hollow Road. Park on the roadside.

Owner: State of New York

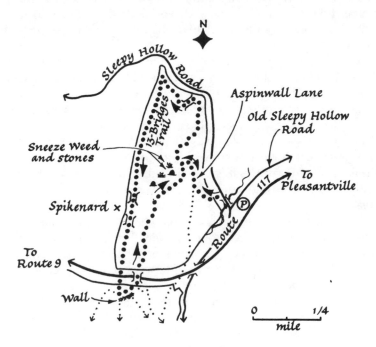

THE ROCKEFELLER FAMILY HAS ALWAYS BEEN
generous in allowing public use of their lands for walking, skiing,
and horseback riding. In the early 1980s, 750 acres of this property
were given to the State of New York, with more to follow. Trails that
were built with horses in mind make very easy and pleasant walking
when they are as well maintained as these. Markers are plastic discs
nailed to the trees.

From your car, walk across Sleepy Hollow Road and enter the
park by a wooden gate. The Pocantico River flows away to the left.
In spring clumps of penstemon, or beardtongue, flower along the
sides of the trail. It is amazing to see bees immerse themselves in
these flowers to reach the nectar deep inside. On the left of the trail
there is a huge rock embraced by the large roots of an oak tree.
Red-bellied woodpeckers frequent these oak trees, giving their
strange mewing calls. The red-bellied woodpecker is a recent emi-
grant to this area from the south. It has a fluorescent red-orange
banner from the top of the head down the neck, but the red on its
belly is so faint it can only be seen when you are holding the bird
in your hand.

At a "T" intersection, turn right. This is the Thirteen Bridges
Trail; the blue discs on the trees bear a "TB" and are numbered.
Late summer is the time when flocks of winter birds form in woodlands such as these. Chickadees, tufted titmice, white-breasted
nuthatches, and downy woodpeckers are constant companions. This
flocking behavior helps the birds find sources of food to share and
also protects individual members from predation, since all are on
the alert. When warblers migrate through in the fall they often join
resident flocks of birds. Any flock is worth investigating for sur-
prises.

At the first bridge there is a large clump of wild ginger. An
unusual wildflower, ragged robin, blooms here in June. It is pink
with frayed-looking petals. In summer jewelweed is abundant.
Many of its leaves show the work of tiny caterpillars which eat the
inner layer of the leaves, leaving tunnels behind. Gory Brook mean-
ders back and forth under the trail, requiring thirteen bridges.

There are many large hemlocks to the left of the trail, a place to
find roosting owls throughout the year. Several small trails branch
off from the main road; continue following the blue discs. In damp
soil near each bridge you'll find clearweed growing. This small
shiny plant has translucent stems, which inspired its name. Clusters

Permits are given for people with carriage horses to drive on the perfect trails of the Rockefeller State Park.

of tiny greenish flowers emerge from the leaf axils. Clearweed is in the nettle family, but it has no stinging hairs.

Another rare wildflower grows on the right side of the trail between two bridges that are close together. This is spikenard, a member of the Aralia family. It has very large double-compound leaves, spikes of small white flowers, and dark purple berries in the fall. Though this is a perennial herbaceous plant, it appears shrublike.

29

After the trail passes under NY 117, walk up a slight grade and turn left. A stone retaining wall on the right has some nice clumps of evergreen ferns growing in crevices between the rocks. One is Christmas fern, a leathery fern common throughout the woods. The other is ebony spleenwort, a small delicate fern which requires limestone soil in order to thrive. It has black wiry stems and can be found at all seasons of the year. In spring the small white flowers of sweet cicely also can be seen on this wall, followed in summer by ribbed seeds which have a faint anise flavor if they are nibbled while they are still green.

Turn left again, still on Thirteen Bridges Trail, and take the overpass back over NY 117. Along the left side of the trail, large stones have been erected as a curb to keep you from plunging down the steep hillside. Among these stones sneezeweed blooms in summer. This yellow flower somewhat resembles black-eyed Susan, but with a higher center cluster of florets. Its name comes from the practice, many years ago, of drying the plant's leaves and using them as a substitute for snuff.

In late summer many small, bright orange chanterelle mushrooms are scattered among the leaf litter. August rains and high humidity encourage the growth of many other varieties of mushrooms here. Most show the teeth marks of chipmunks or the feeding trails of slugs. The plants' gills or pores are often full of tiny insects.

Turn right on Aspinwall Trail, then left to go back to the road and your car.

30

7. Teatown Lake Reservation

Location: Ossining, New York
Distance: 1.6 miles
Access: From the Taconic State Parkway take the exit for NY
    134 west (toward Ossining). Turn at the second right,
    Spring Valley Road. Follow this road about 1 mile. Reser-
    vation buildings and parking lot will be on your right.
Owner: Teatown Lake Reservation

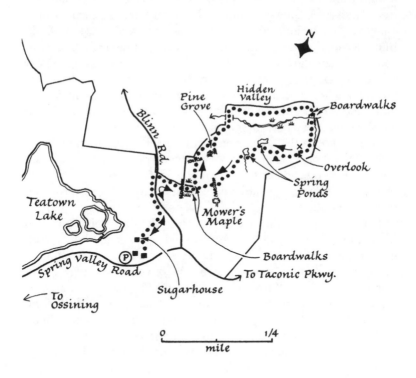

ONE OF THE LARGEST AND FINEST NATURE CEN-
ters in Westchester County, Teatown Lake Reservation was originally a gift from the Swope family. With smaller additions of land
from other generous citizens, Teatown has grown to more than 300
acres. Several fine Tudor-style barns house a museum, its shop,
and the reservation staff. There is a maple syrup house and a small
collection of native animals, notably several species of owls which
cannot be released because of past injuries.

A preserve of this size has many trails. Probably the most popular
one here is the two-mile walk around Teatown Lake. A much less-
trod area containing the Marsh and Meadow and Hidden Valley
Trails offers more variety.

From the parking lot, meander past the sugar house and down
toward Blinn Road. The trail parallels Blinn Road for a few hundred
feet. Trees have grown around old ribbon wire attached to them
many years ago, indicating that this land was once pasture. Cross
Blinn Road at the sign for Marsh and Meadow Trail, and wind
your way along the edge of a swamp and up onto a rocky promontory.
Skeletal cedar trees grow on top of the rocks here; one has a few
green branches. These trees also tell us of once open land in decades
past, since cedars like to grow in bright sunlight. Now the cedars
are overshaded by black birch and maples. As the trail descends a
small hill, notice the green stems of catbrier along the trail on the
right. This thorny plant can make impenetrable thickets, offering
fine winter protection to rabbits and birds. It sometimes bears blue
fruit which is edible by animals, and its new leaves in spring can
be eaten by humans, too.

Through a stone wall, we emerge into the marsh and meadow:
first through a stand of loosestrife beside a rock-and-board walk,
then into a mowed area which is a wave of goldenrod in summer.
Turn left on the trail where a sign directs you to the Pine Grove.
There are a few small trees standing alongside this trail. These are
black walnuts, offspring of the large trees along the wall dividing
the meadows. Take a close look in springtime at their fuzzy, pointed
buds. The tree's large leaf scars look like monkey faces.

Over the next wall we enter an area that is rapidly becoming a
complete snarl of vines punctuated by a few white spruces. The
vines include grapevines with peeling brown bark, bittersweet with
orange berries, and honeysuckle with black berries. The hon-

eysuckle retains some bronze-and-green leaves in winter. Both bittersweet and honeysuckle twine tightly around sapling trees and strangle them. Their virtue lies in their food value for wildlife: berries for birds and browse for deer.

Follow the trail to the right and enter a beautiful, fragrant white pine grove. This grove has been nicely maintained, with dead branches pruned up and piled. You can guess the age of the trees by counting the whorls of branches and adding five for the first years of a tree's growth. These trees appear to be about forty years old. Back into the deciduous woods and up a short slope, we see a large mat of ground cedar, one of the lycopodiums, with its evergreen circles of leaves and its candelabra on top which bear the spores with which lycopodiums, like ferns and mosses, reproduce. These beautiful plants are on the list of protected plants of New York State; they reproduce very slowly and are almost impossible to transplant. Where they find conditions to their liking they grow abundantly, but those conditions are very difficult to copy in artificial situations.

In a short distance you come to an intersection where signs point back the way you have come. Take the trail that turns left here through a nice stand of hemlock and laurel, down a steep hill into Hidden Valley. You cross a brook over a charming Japanese-style bridge and turn right along the base of a rugged rocky slope. The sun pours into this side of the valley. In spring you can actually look up into the faces of numerous red trilliums. Small springs trickle down to feed the swamp and brook. At one point there is a monstrous old yellow birch, mostly hollow but still alive, which leans at a precarious angle out over the swamp. Here in the spring are skunk cabbage, false hellebore, and marsh marigolds in abundance. In winter spectacular ice formations decorate the many small caves and crannies in the rocks.

Keep your nose alert, too — sometimes you can smell a fox! Fox have musk glands which give off an odor similar to that of skunks, but more delicate and not long lasting. The fox can control this odor. They seem to delight in releasing it when they are watching you and know full well you will never see them.

The trail turns sharply to the right over a very nice boardwalk. Along the brook at the end of the walk is a large stand of wild leek and, in season, many clumps of hepatica. The leek sends its leaves up in early spring, looking much like the leaves of lily of the valley. In July these leaves have all died down; then the naked stalks of white starlike flowers appear, to be followed by shiny black seeds.

Now you must climb a very steep hill, beside a rushing brook. Standing among hemlocks at the top, you can look back over the trail you have covered. The trail leads on through a dense stand of laurel, a shrub beautiful not only for its glossy leaves and spectacular flowers, but also for its convoluted trunks and brown bark. In colonial days the hard wood was whittled into various utensils, giving the shrub the name "spoon wood." When you come to an open space be alert for a sign saying "Return" and make a sharp right by a large boulder. Follow the sign through more laurel, to the Spring Ponds Trail. This takes you past several ponds which are called "vernal ponds" because they are usually full of water in spring but dry up in summer. Actually, these are usually full of water in fall and winter, too. They are very active breeding ponds for spring peepers, wood frogs, toads, and salamanders. The second pond also contains a wood duck house, which is occupied each year.

Make a right turn at the Blinn Road sign, crossing the outlet of the second pond, and winding down again to the meadow. Look to your right for a smoky lavender stand of black raspberry bushes. On the left, standing in the wall separating the two meadows, is the largest tree at Teatown. This huge sugar maple has been dubbed the "Mower's Maple," because men mowing these fields by hand may have rested in its shade two hundred years ago. Through the wall, you will find yourself back in the first meadow we entered. Retrace your steps to Blinn Road and back to the main building. The museum and gift shop (various books, hand lenses, other nature-related items) are open all day Tuesday through Saturday and Sunday afternoons.

8. Brooklyn Botanic Garden Research Center

Location: Ossining, New York
Distance: 1.5 miles
Access: From the Taconic State Parkway, exit at NY 134. Go
   east 1.5 miles. The center's entrance is on the left. Parking.
Owner: Brooklyn Botanic Garden

THE BROOKLYN BOTANIC GARDEN MAY SEEM
far from Westchester, but it is the owner of a beautiful county
property of several hundred acres, with more than five miles of
trails open to the public for walking. Known locally as the Kitchawan
Research Lab, the sanctuary's official name is now the Brooklyn
Botanic Garden Research Center. The actual research lab is not
open to the public, but its work lies in the field of plant pathology,
and its scientists are particularly interested in the effects of air
pollution on plants and the development of plants that are pollution-
resistant. In this very attractive building near the parking lot there
is a plant shop, stocked and manned by the center's volunteers.
The shop is open Tuesday through Saturday. It is a fine place to
visit and a good source of interesting plants for your home.

Walk left from the entrance sign in the parking lot along a dirt
road which leads to a pond. The pond is not on the Kitchawan
property but is owned by the Misses Catherine and Elizabeth Van
Brunt, who donated the Kitchawan land and who still live on the
farm adjacent to it. Without violating the Van Brunt's privacy, we
can look for birds in the shrubs around the edges of this pond.

Turn right at the sign for Little Brook Nature Trail. Called a
"labeled nature trail," it is the work of an Eagle Scout. His labeling
has now fallen into disrepair except for a few fern and tree names.
One large sign on the left discusses the characteristics and demise
of the American chestnut, former glory of the Northeastern woods.
Most of the old weathered stumps seen in our woodlands are
chestnut stumps. They can be recognized by their gray color and
by the vertical striation of their wood. Often the stumps support
beautiful lichen and moss colonies.

When these trees died of a fungus imported from China, local
residents cut them quickly for building material and fence posts,
so the total resource was not lost. Some of that fencing is still in
existence. Research on this chestnut fungus is continuing. There is
hope that a control will be found before we lose all of the sprouts
that still come up from the trees' old roots.

Little Brook would appear to be a "young" brook — the sides of
its bed are very steep and no flood plain has developed. The brook
flows from the pond we passed earlier to the Croton Reservoir,
which borders this property.

The presence of many reservoirs in Westchester affects what use may be made of our waters. Any pond or lake whose outlet goes into a reservoir is under the control of both the State and the City of New York. If you wish to put chemicals into such a pond to control algae or fish or for any other reason, you have to get permission from both the state and city. This is really an excellent way to keep chemicals out of our waters. I wonder if many city dwellers realize how dependent they are on Westchester for their water.

Some of the most visible animal traces along these trails are mole tunnels, many with holes where the animals must have emerged for nightly forays. Moles do not hibernate. They spend the winter down below the frost line, tunneling for earthworms, their major food, and for other burrowing creatures such as the grubs of May and Japanese beetles.

Moles have the most beautiful fur of any mammal. (Don't the kings in fairy stories sometimes wear capes of moleskin?) One characteristic of this fantastic fur reflects the animal's burrowing lifestyle. Unlike other mammal fur which stands on end if stroked backward, the mole's fur lies flat no matter which way it is stroked. If, as a mole tunnels along, it comes to a large rock or root which it cannot get around, it must back up. But the tunnel is the same size as its body. If its fur stood on end when it backed up, it would be constantly full of dirt. But the mole's fur always lies flat. This gives it the feel of velvet.

Another animal that may make itself known to you in these woods is the ruffed grouse or partridge. When alarmed, these large birds take off with a thunder of wings. The ruffed grouse is our woodland "chicken," spending most of its time on the ground in search of food. Usually it roosts on the ground, or low in thickets. As winter approaches, the grouse grows small bristly feathers along its toes, providing it with winter snowshoes. Its tracks in snow are almost toe-to-heel — very close together. If the ground is snow covered and food among the leaves is hard to find, grouse will eat buds from shrubs and trees.

When, in fall or spring, you hear a sound like a distant motorcycle engine trying in vain to start, you may be hearing the drumming of a male grouse. The bird stands on a log and fans the air with his wings so quickly that a drumming sound is produced. He does not actually hit the log with his wings. The sound assumes the function of song in other birds, serving to identify a territory and to attract a mate. The bird may be closer to you than you think. But it's very hard to see a grouse drumming.

When you come to a sign directing you to the Beech Grove, take that turn to the left. There are many individual beeches in Westchester woods, but in this spot beech is the dominant tree. Note how abundant the young ones are, each waiting for a chance to replace a parent tree. Not many trees in our forest can grow in shade this way.

The trail through the beech grove continues onto the watershed property and eventually to Croton reservoir. This land is not open to the public, so we must glimpse the reservoir through trees, turn around, and go back to the sign directing us up the Red Oak Trail to Jackson Hill.

Some of the roots, rocks, and logs along this trail sport beautiful growths of a moss called delicate fern moss, since its leaves resemble ferns. It has taken at least 50 years for moss to cover these rocks, so be careful not to disturb it. Moss has great value as a ground cover and in the preparation of soil for future, more "advanced," plant growth, because it adds organic material to thin soils.

In muddy places look for deer prints. The hemlock grove along the ridge to your right provides good shelter for deer.

The Red Oak Trail goes gradually up the slope of Jackson Hill. At the top you will see a place where some wood has been cut. The drive for alternate energy sources makes it necessary for woodland owners to keep a sharp eye out for "wood rustlers."

Follow the wide truck path to the next intersection. A right turn here will take you back to the laboratory and the parking lot.

9. Turkey Mountain Park

Location: Yorktown, New York
Distance: 2.5 miles
Access: From the intersection of NY 202, NY 35, and NY 118 in the center of Yorktown Heights, go south on NY 118 for 2 miles. Look for the park's entrance sign on the right. People driving north on NY 118 from its intersection with NY 129 will find the entrance on their left. Parking.
Owner: Town of Yorktown

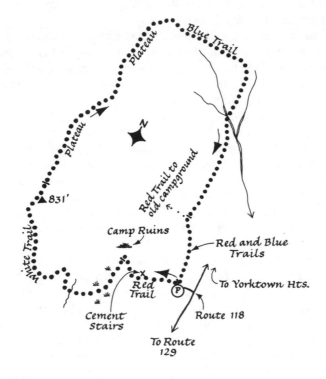

TURKEY MOUNTAIN WAS PRESERVED THROUGH
the efforts of concerned citizens who recognized its value. Though
the park's problems — principally vandalism and fires — are still
many, the appeal of its woodpeckers, bluebirds, impressive rock
formations, and beautiful views far outweigh them.

Leave your car in the parking lot, and don't be in a rush to get
to "the top." There is a lot to see at lower elevations. Bear left from
the parking area, and take the Red Trail cut through some rocks.
Admire the huge boulders with their miniature gardens of moss,
blueberry, and partridge berry. Among the rocks bloom lovely lady's
slippers, native orchids more beautiful than expensive hothouse
varieties (please don't pick them). Some of these massive boulders
sport a lush growth of rocktripe, a lichen that is edible if you like
to chew old leather. It does have a faint mushroom flavor and
perhaps in an emergency could taste good.

The old cement stairs and foundations which you will see in the
park are leftovers from the 1930s, when this was a summer camp.
Follow the Red Trail past these remains, then turn left on the White
Trail. The path goes through moist woods and over a small stream.
The common shrub of this area is spice bush, whose red shiny
berries are a prime food for robins and other thrushes during migration. Ferns of several varieties decorate the forest floor.

There are many worm castings in the moist soil of the trail near
the brook. Worms are vital in the creation of soil. They are active
at night, pulling down into their holes decaying leaves and other
plant matter, eating them, and releasing many of the plants' minerals
into the soil. At the same time they create air spaces in the soil
(even plant roots need air) and tunnels that rain can go into, helping
the water soak in rather than run off.

Where small trees have fallen across the trail they have formed
natural dams, holding the soil as it washes down the trail and helping
to keep it out of the stream. The same principle has been used by
man in building "check-dams" on the steep parts of the trail. Listen
for drumming woodpeckers. Woodpeckers use this drumming to
define their nesting territories and to attract mates. The more reso-
nant the hollow tree, the louder the noise. Anyone who has heard a
woodpecker drumming on a house drainpipe will appreciate their
staying in the woods. Woodpeckers often make holes in houses,
too. The latest theory to explain this is that they hear tiny sounds

made by electrical wiring within house walls and think the sounds are insects. Woodpeckers have very sensitive ears and locate wood-boring insects by hearing them.

It soon becomes apparent that most people using Turkey Mountain are on their way to the top. This White Trail is very well packed, and alignment of parts of it have been altered to take advantage of rocks and to eliminate erosion. When you stop to catch your breath, be sure to turn and look back. The views along the way are nice, and you will be impressed by how high you already are.

The view from the summit (831 feet) is spectacular: the Croton Reservoir and Dam, the Hudson River, Maryknoll's Oriental towers, and New York City's skyline far in the distance. This is a good place to sit and look for hawks. Bluebirds nest here, along with field sparrows and prairie warblers. The summit's plants show the effect of high winds; they are mostly stunted and twisted into interesting shapes. Some of them, such as the little scrub oaks, cannot be found at lower elevations. There are many blueberry bushes and also deerberry, which does not have a fruit edible for humans. Clumps of pale corydalis huddle in rock crevices.

As we start onto the Blue Trail we see evidence that fire has been a way of life to this mountain. Fire is a very frightening phenomenon; once I was on the mountain just a few hours before a fire, and I was very glad not to have been trapped there. Today forest management includes the use of fire to keep ground material from building up to such depths that a fire would kill even the biggest trees. Fires that burn quickly will often take the underbrush but leave big trees alive. After a fire new plants invade — grasses, wildflowers, blackberries. The animals that have been able to flee and survive benefit from this.

The Blue Trail goes eastward along the ridge. Different views present themselves. Much of the area is open and grassy, and there are more interesting plants, such as the bastard toadflax, a parasite on the roots of other plants. There are two turns to be made — just remember to take the right-hand turn at each opportunity. If you come out under a power line, you have missed one turn. There is a very steep descent on this trail, so watch your footing. It helps to place your feet sideways against the slope, to keep from pitching forward.

Many wonderful rock formations border this trail. As the ancient

41

glaciers scoured smooth the top of the mountain, they broke rocks from the south side and left them in giant rockpiles. The call of the pileated woodpecker echoes from these cliffs, a dramatic setting for the Northeast's most dramatic woodpecker.

The Blue Trail is considerably longer than the White and affords us a chance to enjoy the lower slopes of the mountain. The Blue Trail comes to the Red Trail, where a left-hand turn takes us back to the parking lot. The right turn wanders around the old camp area. The Blue Trail was laid out and built by the first Walkabout class, an alternative high school in Yorktown, as a community service. This park has also afforded summer employment for other local young people.

Recently wild turkeys have been reported in this vicinity. Perhaps that wily bird will soon be seen again within the park that bears its name.

10. Choate Sanctuary

Location: Chappaqua, New York
Distance: 0.75 mile
Access: From the Saw Mill River Parkway take the NY 133/ Mt. Kisco exit, and go left (west) on NY 133 (Millwood Road) 0.5 mile to Crow Hill Road on the right, opposite the Presbyterian church. The sanctuary sign is 100 feet farther north on Crow Hill Road. Small parking area, or use church lot.
Owner: Saw Mill River Audubon Society

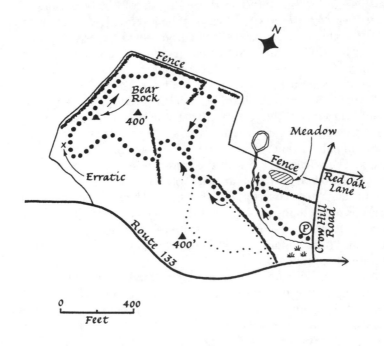

YOU CAN SEE DEER, FOX, WEASEL, AND MANY
different birds in this 28-acre sanctuary, even though the traffic
noises from NY 133 are ever present. Choate is an unexpected little
oasis amid the suburbanization of Chappaqua.

Before you begin your walk, take time to register your name in
the box provided on a tree near the trail entrance. This helps the
Audubon Society keep track of the sanctuary's use. As you walk
through the dogwood thicket (one of the shrub dogwoods, *Cornus
racemosa* or gray-stemmed dogwood), be alert in the fall for flocks
of birds feeding on the shrub's white berries. These fruits are highly
favored by migrants.

Briefly leave the main trail by going straight ahead over a stone
wall and bearing right into a small meadow. This is the only open
land in the sanctuary except for the marsh at the corner of NY 133
and Crow Hill Road (which is full of sweet flag, by the way, not
cattails; no brown cigar-shaped seed heads can be seen, and the
sweet flag flower is down low among the leaves). This meadow has
lots of mountain mint, yarrow, goldenrod — and butterflies! It must
be cut by hand each fall to prevent its growing into forest. There
is no easy way to bring a machine in here, so volunteers use old-
fashioned tools such as scythes for the work.

Return through the wall to the trail, turn right, and walk over a
small bridge above the stream. The stream originates in a pond off
the property and runs all year. Tracks of raccoons are usually evident. In cold weather winter wrens frequent the stream's brushy
edges. The willow tree beside the bridge has sent up many small
branches since it first leaned, making a fence effect.

The moss that covers these rocks has taken at least 50 years,
perhaps more, to grow — a long life for such a seemingly insignifi-
cant life form. Jewelweed is abundant beside the bridge in summer
and fall. Hummingbirds in fall migration almost always appear at
clumps of jewelweed.

As you follow along the trail beyond the bridge, you will see
many large, dead spice bushes. Several years ago they were seriously
infected by a fungus disease. The Carey Arboretum of the New
York Botanical Garden suggested that all affected plants be cut and
burned. The Audubon Society caretakers felt that this was not only
undesirable but also impossible, so the cure was left to nature. Most
of the spice bushes have resprouted.

On hot summer days cicadas will be trilling. Annual cicadas,

44

which spend just one year underground as nymphs, take their six weeks in the sun to reproduce. Then they die. Every 17 years a different kind of cicada may appear. This one is slightly smaller and is black and orange (in contrast to the brown and green of our annual drummer). The seventeen-year cicada's call is much quieter and sounds like a distant generator. The incredible sounds which both cicadas emit are made by tympanums, or drumheads of skin, on the sides of their muscularly vibrated abdomens. It is the males who "call." People sometimes refer to these insects as locusts, but the real locust is a kind of grasshopper well known for the damage it can do to crops, especially in dry areas.

Through the wall, turn right, and at the next intersection bear right and step over a log. Christmas fern forms a dark evergreen bound to the path. On the right, baneberry or doll's eyes grows, with fluffy white flowers in spring and white berries in fall. These berries are beautiful but poisonous. At the "Y," bear left past a large clump of shining club moss. This sanctuary has a number of the lycopodiums, the near relatives of mosses and ferns. With a hand lens you can see the clam-shaped spore cases between the leaves of the club moss.

It's a green, green world — but the shades of green are so variable! Where the trail bends left in a little distance, you can see two forms of very different greens on the right — Christmas fern and marginal shield fern, the one dark and glossy, the other almost turquoise and matt-finished. By the trail on the left is a growth of yellow-green grass, probably one of the plants the deer enjoy eating here.

Up the hill and through another wall, look on the left for the skeletal cedars in the wall. Most of the large trees in this sanctuary are oaks. During gypsy moth infestations they are apt to be leafless in July; their recovery during off years is apparent.

As you go over the crest of this hill, you will be constantly aware of the noise from NY 133. Go downhill again, passing New York fern of a bright yellow-green. Its leaflets taper at both ends of the stem. Snakeroot usually blooms here in early summer, by a long log on the ground. Look carefully at this point to see an interesting association of insects — aphids with their beaks in the stem of the plant and ants clustered around the aphids. The ants guard the aphids from predators and benefit by drinking the "honeydew" that the aphids exude from their abdomens. Some ants will even take these aphids into their underground homes for winter protection.

45

You now approach a huge erratic — a boulder that stands alone, dropped here by the glacier — which makes a dramatic contribution to the landscape. Along the right side of this trail as it winds down between two ridges, one rock looks to me like a bear's head. Do you believe rocks have spirits? Three times I have photographed this bear's head rock, and three times the film came out blank.

Up a little hill, and down again, and you will see a well-patronized woodpecker luncheon spot, a black birch stump full of holes. What will happen to our woodpeckers when there are no dead trees left standing? It's a good thing all trees are not suitable for firewood. We need more consumer education, so everyone with a wood-burning stove will know which trees to take and why to leave some dead wood standing.

Walking quietly pays off. If you walk with friends, try to talk later so you can observe the kind of thing I was once lucky enough to see here. While I was quietly looking up a pretty plant called spreading dogbane in my wildflower guide, a cabbage butterfly came gliding along and lit on a dogbane flower. All at once the butterfly began flapping madly, not going anywhere. Close examination showed an ambush bug had driven its sharp stiletto right between the butterfly's green eyes. Suddenly there was a buzzing, and a white-faced hornet proceeded to grab the prize away from the ambush bug. Carrying it up to a low tree branch, the hornet cut off the butterfly's wings, rolled up the rest, then flew off with it, probably to a nest to feed some hungry hornet larva. An incredible performance, seen only because I had been still.

Two conspicuous lycopodiums grow along this path, ground cedar and ground pine, *L. complanatum* and *L. obscurum* respectively. A third and much less common one, *L. annotinum*, appears sparsely. At a "Y" in the trail, with a patch of Indian tobacco in the path (*Lobelia inflata*, with lavender flowers in spikes), bear left, then left again, to go back to the sanctuary entrance. If you continue straight you will be on the sanctuary's second loop. Marked by white with a red dot, it has some spectacular cliffs and is slightly shorter than the walk just described.

46

11. Gedney Brook Sanctuary

Location: Chappaqua, New York

Distance: 1.5 miles

Access: From the Saw Mill River Parkway, exit at NY 133,
Mt. Kisco. Go west on NY 133 for 2 miles to a stop light at
Seven Bridges Road. Continue on NY 133 for 1 mile to
Woodmill Road on the left. The sanctuary is off a stub road
on the right near the end of Woodmill. Roadside parking.

Owner: Saw Mill River Audubon Society

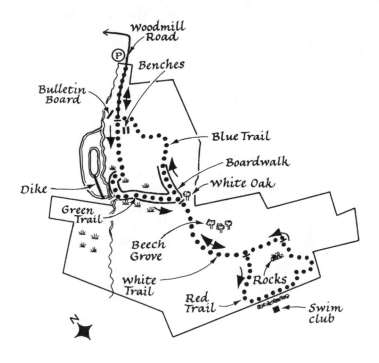

SIXTY ACRES OF LOWLAND AND RIDGE, SWAMP,
and beautiful rock formations, this sanctuary supports a herd of
seven deer. It is also a place where you can see all the woodpeckers
to be found in this part of the country: downy, hairy, flicker, red-bellied, and pileated.

Leave your car on the road, being careful not to block any drive-
ways. After you have walked a short distance into the sanctuary,
you will see a bulletin board on the right. A map is available in the
nearby registry box. Continue straight through an area that has
been cleared of trees in an effort to introduce another habitat to
this mainly forested land. Many wildflowers and grasses grow in
this more open area, providing food for varieties of birds and mammals which otherwise would not be here, such as rabbits and song
sparrows. At the end of this fairly wide path, turn right onto a
boardwalk. You are now on the Green Trail. A slow approach to
the pond's edge may result in your seeing a wood duck, mallard,
or spotted sandpiper. Many birds can be found in this swampy area
at all seasons.

What is the difference between a swamp and a marsh? A swamp
has trees, while a marsh has none. In spring this swamp boasts a
magnificent growth of skunk cabbage. Tussock sedges, royal ferns,
and marsh marigolds follow in season. This pond is man-made,
and not very successful. The brook which feeds into it has a low
gradient of flow. As a result, siltation is rapid, and in summer most
of the pond on this side is a mud flat. Where the boardwalk parallels
the brook, you will see the remains of a dike built to keep the brook
out of the pond. Periodic high water and the tunneling of muskrats
have made this dike impossible to maintain. A dam to deepen the
water cannot be built, for at the upper reaches of the brook are
springs used to provide bottled water. Backing the water up into
these springs would infringe on the rights of their owners.

At the "T" intersection there is a bridge over the brook. You can
cross over to get a better look at the pond, but the trails on the far
side are on private land, so return and continue on the boardwalk.
In summer cinnamon ferns here resemble a tropical jungle, and
swamp azaleas fill the air with their perfume.

All the way along these trails, dead trees are evident. The
sanctuary's policy is to let dead wood alone, except to move it off
the trails. That is why so many woodpeckers come here. The red-bellied woodpecker is one of the newest birds to invade our region

48

from the south, and it is staying year-round. Twenty years ago, the pileated, our biggest woodpecker, was rarely seen in Westchester. Now the increase in maturing forest with carpenter ant-infested trees has encouraged the presence of this crow-sized bird.

Where the boardwalk makes a sharp left-hand turn, bear right onto the White Trail. This leads through a beautiful beech grove to a higher area. Spring beauties carpet the forest in April. Take a white-with-red-dot trail branching off to the right. This is a younger forest, with occasional stumps and logs of long-dead American chestnut. Soon the trail bears left and parallels a stone wall, with swamp on the other side. You may catch sight of some of the spring houses back in the woods. The path along the wall catches an extra thick leaf fall, and walking it is like walking on a mattress. Rocks in the wall are beautiful with lichen.

As you have seen, much of the sanctuary consists of deciduous woods. This word comes from the Latin "caducus," meaning inclined to fall, or transitory. The shortening days of autumn are the key to the dropping of leaves. Short days mean that the trees, using the energy of the sun, water, and nutrients from the soil, combined with the green chlorophyll in their leaves, can no longer manufacture food. The green pigment then breaks down, and the reds, yellows, and other pigments which were masked by that green become visible.

When sap ceases to flow from stem to leaf, a sealing-off layer of cork called the abcission layer is formed, and eventually the leaf drops to the ground. Trees such as beeches and oaks, which retain their leaves much of the winter, have only partial abcission layers. Their old leaves sometimes hang on until they are pushed off by the new growth in spring.

Most of the leaves that drop have at least small holes in them. The energy created by the tree serves to feed a great many small creatures, including aphids, caterpillars, and leaf hoppers. Once the leaves reach the ground they will be slowly consumed by other herbivores. Among these are worms, springtails, and sow bugs.

The trail winds up into the highlands, past some nice rock formations. Turn left when you reach a wider path, and go back to the start of the White Trail. Just before meeting the Green Trail again, look on the bark of a large white oak on your right for bark beetles. These cousins of fireflies are evident in the bark crevices on all but the coldest days of winter.

Turn right on the Green Trail then bear right at a "Y" intersection. Now you are on the Blue Trail. It leads through a very moist valley, where unusually fine wildflower displays can be seen. Sometimes deer can be spotted on the tops of the hills above this ravine. One of the things they seem to enjoy eating in April is the flower of the Dutchman's breeches, whose rejected leaves are abundant here. One huge dead oak has fallen across the trail, making a natural bridge. This tree should be with us a long time, inasmuch as most of it is not touching the ground, where it would absorb moisture, speeding decay. It will be interesting to see what fungi appear on this trunk as time goes by.

The Blue Trail bears left past another fallen giant. Up this slope are several kinds of vines: grapevine, honeysuckle, woodbine, and — unfortunately — Oriental bittersweet, which must be constantly battled. Along the top are some plants we would normally expect to see lower down in more moist conditions, such as jack-in-the-pulpit and spice bush. There must be water under there somewhere! Downslope again, past spring carpets of Canada mayflower and evergreen Christmas fern, there is a large patch of wild leek on the right. Its leaves, resembling lily of the valley, come up in early spring. In June they die down, to be followed in July by naked flower stalks with typical onion flowers and shiny black seeds. In the south this plant is known as ramps, and is commonly eaten. The leaves are quite tasty, raw in salads or as an ingredient in leek soup.

The Blue Trail brings you back near your point of entry. Turn right. There are several other trails to be explored in Gedney Brook. This is an excellent place for birding, especially during migration. Over a ten-year period of banding birds with Federal leg bands, more than 90 species have been encountered in this sanctuary.

12. Pinecliff Sanctuary

Location: Chappaqua, New York

Distance: 0.5 mile

Access: Pinecliff Sanctuary is at the end of Pinecliff Road, off
NY 120. Pinecliff Road is the third street on the left beyond
the Quaker Meeting House, or the third street on the right
after the Saw Mill River Parkway overpass in the village
center. Park on the roadside.

Owner: Saw Mill River Audubon Society

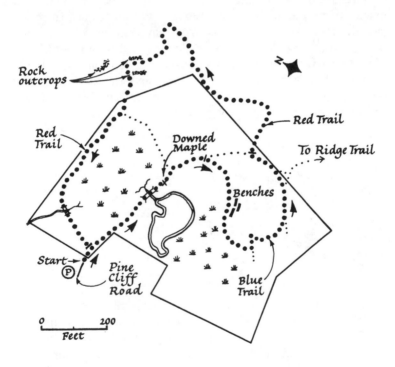

SAW MILL RIVER AUDUBON SOCIETY IS PRIVI-
ledged to own several small sanctuaries, mostly in the Chappaqua
area, which serve a special function as protected wetlands. Pinecliff
Sanctuary is one of these. Wetlands are very important in maintain-
ing underground water tables and soaking up excessive rainwater.
While this Audubon sanctuary is small (approximately seven acres),
it is important because it adjoins larger green spaces and provides
a variety of habitat for several interesting groups of animals.

The entrance path leads between two ponds, one open and one
almost a swamp with many trees. The open pond sports an incredible
variety of water life, especially insects and amphibians. If you want
to investigate this, take a kitchen strainer and a small (preferably
white) pan with you. Put some water in the pan, then scoop with
the strainer, trying to get muck from the pond's bottom. Dump the
muck on the ground and sort through. Put anything that moves
into the clear water in the pan. You may find tadpoles of toads,
frogs, and salamanders (salamander tadpoles can be identified because they have external gills and legs from a very early stage). The
nymphs of dragonflies and damselflies, and the larva and adult
stages of giant water beetles, water scorpions, and backswimmers
will probably be among those present.

The unusual wealth of this pond is the result of its containing
no fish. There are few predators on the pond's insect and amphibian
life. Several years ago there were many goldfish, but they have
disappeared. Goldfish are not native to this country. Sometimes
people who tire of watching goldfish swim around in a bowl will
mistakenly release them in ponds such as this. Goldfish are really
fancy carp. They are bottom feeders and tend to keep a pond riled
up and muddy, cutting down the oxygen supply for other life forms.

52

So please, if you tire of your goldfish, give them to someone else. Don't release them in a local pond.

Most of the open pond's surface is covered by a green film — but this is not algae. It is a tiny flowering plant called duckweed. Two kinds, Lemna and Wolffia, can be seen. These are the world's smallest flowering plants, though flowers are rarely seen, as the plants increase by vegetative division. In the hand they feel and look like green sand. Duckweed is the favorite food of the beautiful wood duck. A pair frequents this area in spring, the female shielding her ducklings in the tangled vegetation of the swampy pond. Wood ducks nest in hollow trees. A number of dead trees with old woodpecker holes that are ideal for these ducks rise from the swampy pond and the back of the open pond. Green herons and kingfishers also visit the open pond.

As you continue on the trail away from the ponds, your path will be crossed by a downed red maple. This is not poor trail maintenance. The tree has been left on purpose to discourage motorcyclists from crossing the sanctuary on their way to the Ridge Trail, which runs along the Saw Mill River Parkway all the way to Roaring Brook Road. It's easy to step over the tree. Continue on until you see a blue marker on a tree to your right. Turn right onto the Blue Trail. After a short walk through the woodland you will come upon three benches, sited so that you may sit and overlook the swampy back of the open pond.

These benches and the Blue Trail were installed a few years ago by a special education class from the Todd School in Briarcliff. They provide a pleasant vantage point amid the mosses and ferns for observing activity at the back of the pond and around its dead trees. Great crested flycatchers frequent this area in spring, probably nesting in one of the tree holes. The male bird calls with a raucous "Weep!" sound. Mosses here are emerald, and ferns green and feathery. One of Westchester's less common plants, the whorled wood aster, is abundant here, too. Check your wildflower book for its leaf structure, and you will recognize it easily.

The Blue Trail continues along the edge of the swamp, then swings to the left up the hill. It turns to the right through some nice rock outcroppings and leads down through a cluster of large beech trees to intersect the entrance trail. Make a left here, and take the Red Trail, which branches off to your right.

One of the most elusive of our amphibians is the spring peeper, a tiny tree frog about one inch long. Its shrill voice in early spring, when it is in the pond for mating, can be deafening. Spotting a peeper is a challenge, even though there are many in this woodland. On almost any moist day, a tiny creature may hop away from your feet. Look quickly now — it matches the leaves — and you'll see a peeper. Peepers do not stray far from their breeding grounds in summer.

Follow the Red Trail over a small ridge and into a little valley, bearing left, then right up the ridge on the other side. A fine stand of bugbane grows here. Bugbane has other names, including black cohosh and black snakeroot. Why it is called bugbane is a mystery, because "bugs" seem to love its flowers. The scent of these white spikes is certainly not very pleasant for people. Their form, however, pleases the eye, and the seed pods which follow are also very handsome, round and brown, and persisting far into the winter.

As the Red Trail tops the hill, there are handsome formations of gneiss rock on your left. These rocks, folded and squished together, look like a lot of gray whipped cream. They provide interesting nooks and crannies for nesting chipmunks.

The Red Trail continues down the hill and proceeds along the back of the swampy pond. A fascinating ash tree provides a bridge. Long ago this tree was bent and broken, but it still lives, projecting a large trunk from a supporting stone wall high into the air.

There is a cultivated note along this trail too — a huge patch of pachysandra. This ubiquitous suburbia ground cover probably got its start from some strands dumped by a gardener, and the rich woodland soil and moist conditions have encouraged it to flourish. Trilliums, jack-in-the-pulpits, and ferns poke their way through the pachysandra, in spring.

The trail continues, skirting the wetland, past upturned root systems and large tulip trees. Cross an outlet on some rocks, and you will find yourself passing the neighborhood brush pile, on your way back to your car.

Note: The East Hudson Parkway Authority owns much of the land to the east of this sanctuary. The Ridge Trail, which runs along their land, is very interesting, should you wish to walk for a longer distance (perhaps a mile to Roaring Brook Road and another mile back). Spring flowers such as ginger, blue cohosh, and trillium are especially rewarding on that trail.

54

13. Muscoot Farm Park

Location: Somers, New York
Distance: 2.5 miles
Access: From I-684 or Saw Mill River Parkway, exit at Cross
    River/Katonah. Follow NY 35 west to its intersection with
    NY 100. Turn left (south) and drive 1 mile to the sanctuary
    entrance on the right. Parking.
Owner: County of Westchester

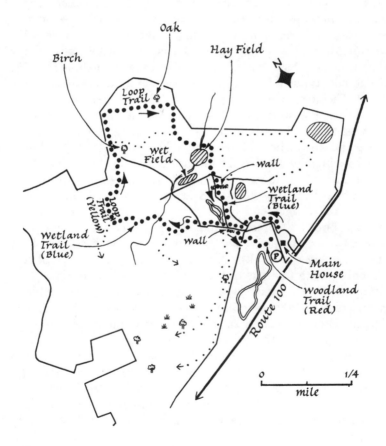

IN MAY THE EDGES OF THE FIRST MUSCOOT ROAD
you walk on are so full of birds you will not want to move along.
Yellow warblers, barn swallows, house wrens, and orioles all frequent the shrubs and trees here. Many bird houses have been erected
by a 4-H club, and bluebirds are almost always visible. This
sanctuary's more than seven hundred acres encompass a turn-of-the-
century farm complete with cows, pigs, chickens, goats, and sheep.
Add woodlands and wetlands to that, and you have a variety of
habitats that is unique in Westchester.

Begin your walk by following the dirt road from the parking area
past the cow pasture. In addition to birds, you may see box turtles
crossing from one field to another. This old farm road passes the
end of a pond which is becoming very swampy, with red maples
and wetland shrubs growing on the hummocks. One warm May
morning while I was walking this section, I heard a soft mewling
sound and splashing in the water. I stood quietly watching the edge
of the pond, and a fawn appeared, wandering uncertainly in the
water. Then I realized its mother was there, too, feeding on water
plants. The doe soon spotted me and, tail high in the air, ran off,
leaving her fawn behind in the water. When I returned this way, it
was gone. The instinct of the fawn to hide when its mother leaves
is deeply ingrained and saves it from danger.

You are now on the Yellow Trail. Continue straight into the woods.
Notice how the bird population changes. Ovenbirds, wood thrushes,
veeries, and towhees are heard, if not always seen. Both veeries
and ovenbirds nest on the ground. When you see one of these birds
suddenly fly up before you, it pays to spend a few minutes looking
under the edges of small shrubs and ground cover. This is almost
the only way to find one of their hidden nests. The *Breeding Bird
Atlas of the State of New York*, a five-year study done by the combined
efforts of the Federated Bird Clubs of New York, the National
Audubon Society, and the state Department of Environmental Conservation, indicates that as many as 64 species nest in this park.

Continue straight on the Yellow Trail. Hay-scented ferns are abundant on the left. These light yellow-green ferns are covered with
silver fuzz. They have a pleasant smell when they are crushed.

Turn right on the Blue Trail. Where this trail crosses a small
stream the woodland is almost one hundred percent black birch.
In May you will see thousands of tiny black birch seedlings all along

56

the sides of the trail. They can grow in very difficult places, such as the crevices of rocks. One of the principal low shrubs along this trail is huckleberry. In spring you can separate it from lowbush blueberry by the golden resin dots on the back of its leaves. When the fruit is present it is black and has many more and larger seeds than the blueberry.

At the end of the Blue Trail, turn right on the Yellow Trail once again. After you pass through a wall, look for a pointed rock on the right. Here is a beautiful garden of maidenhair fern, bugbane, and two of the tick trefoils — naked flowered (so called because the flowers grow on a stalk without leaves) and pointed leaved, with the flower stalk rising from the center of the leaf whorl. This trail leads you through an area that was lumbered during the early 1980s. The increased light level has made the area perfect for such plants as blackberries. Yellow star grass blooms in the trail in spring.

As the Yellow Trail approaches an open field, look to your right for an unusual black birch with very low, spreading branches. Turn right, still on the Yellow Trail. By a large black birch tree on the left is a patch of wood betony, also called lousewort. "Wort" is an old English word meaning plant. Many plants were named for the properties they were thought to have. In the case of lousewort, it was thought that if sheep ate the plant they would not have lice.

There are several unusually large trees along this trail. One is a double shagbark hickory. Another is a white oak that must have been standing when the wall was built two hundred years ago. Muscoot is one of the best places to see white-tailed deer, because their population is large and the human invasion of their woodlands is small. This area is quite open, as the deer have browsed many of the shrubs and herbaceous plants, including, in winter, the many clumps of Christmas fern.

The Yellow Trail emerges into a hayfield. Walk diagonally to the right across the field to find a crossing over the stream. The wet field to your right beyond the crossing is very interesting. In spring plants flower here such as swamp saxifrage and golden ragwort (a plant with ragged-looking leaves), with blue flag along the edge of the stream. Later in the summer the wild bergamot, or bee balm, colors the field with lavender.

Cross the stone wall to your left and follow the trail along the edge of the pond. There are many painted turtles in this pond;

sometimes as many as 50 little heads stick up out of the water. Green herons nest nearby, and red-winged blackbirds complain about your presence. Both yellow-throated and white-eyed vireos nest in the trees near the pond. In the hillside field to the left above the pond, brown thrashers and prairie warblers sing.

At the "T" intersection, turn left, then right at an opening in the wall. This trail brings you back through a woodland that is almost entirely made up of sugar maple. The Museum and Laboratory for Archeology, a Westchester group, has a dig nearby. They are quartered at Muscoot and each year invite people to come with any artifacts they may have found, for identification. There is a lot to see around Muscoot's buildings, with special events relating to farm life offered on a regular basis.

14. Eugene and Agnes Meyer Nature Preserve

Location: Mt. Kisco, New York

Distance: 1.5 miles

Access: Exit I-684 at Armonk. On NY 22, go north 0.6 mile to a blinking light. Turn left onto Cox Avenue. Bear right at a "Y" intersection onto Byram Lake Road. At 1.8 miles turn left onto Oregon Road. Drive 0.1 mile to a small parking area on the right.

Owner: The Nature Conservancy

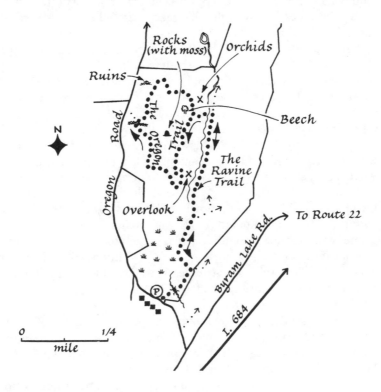

WITHIN ITS BORDERS THE MEYER PRESERVE offers a great variety of habitat — deciduous forest, pine groves, rocky cliffs, ravines, and fields. In every season you can find flowers, mosses, trees, and birds to enjoy.

Follow the trail at the left corner of the parking area. Wood chips are pleasant to walk on, but their main virtue is the prevention of trail erosion, especially in damp areas. Where a bridge crosses a stream, marsh marigolds raise their golden flowers in early spring. By July many of the spring flowers have completely disappeared, leaves and all. In late summer flashy red cardinal flowers bloom here.

At the registry box you can sign in and pick up a map. Continue along the Blue Trail. In summer deer flies will probably accompany you. These very pretty flies, with patterned black and white wings and golden eyes, can give an unpleasant stab with their stiletto mouths. They like to get into people's hair. The larvae of these flies live in the water, so you will often meet them where trails parallel streams and swamps.

Walk on through a small hemlock forest, and bear left onto the Orange Trail. White violets are spattered along both sides of this path, flowering in early spring and keeping their heart-shaped leaves all summer. The stream beside the trail rushes at times of high water, but in summer it gurgles along from pool to pool. Louisiana water thrushes conceal their nests in the overhanging roots and rocks. Their loud calls echo down the ravine. In cold weather, winter wrens search for food among fallen logs in this stream, stretching their tiny legs to the fullest to observe intruders.

Turn left across the brook onto the Yellow Trail (also known as the Oregon Trail). In May you will see blooming among these rocks two of the most uncommon of our wild orchids, the yellow lady's slipper and the showy orchis. There is ginger, too, and broad beech fern. Halfway up the hill, turn left at the "T" intersection. Sunlight dances off spiderwebs in small clearings. Leafrollers, small green translucent caterpillars, can be found on the sweet pepperbush and witch hazel here in spring.

Look among the many rock outcroppings for cushions of moss. The rounded, pale green mounds are aptly called pincushion moss. Sometimes chipmunks tear them apart to get soft material for the linings of their nests. The trail turns left for a short walk to an overlook. With all the trees in full leaf, in summer there is not much to see. Unfortunately there is much to hear, since at this point you are standing high above I-684.

The Yellow Trail goes on through open deciduous woodland, over a series of low ridges, and into valleys. Where you pass through a stone wall, a trail to the left goes on to Oregon Road and beyond the road to large fields that are part of this sanctuary. Continue on the Yellow Trail, turning right.

Summer is a very quiet time for birds. Even in the early mornings, there is little song. Robins and cardinals, which raise more than one brood of young, still sing even into August, but with most other species the young are on their own. Because the adults are going through a post-breeding molt and no longer defending nest territories, they do not sing. This makes them harder to spot, especially in leafy woods.

Tall trees and distant views are part of Meyer's charm.

Yellow Lady-Slipper

The trail passes through a fragrant pine grove and into an area that was once an estate. Ruined walls, a chimney, and cultivated plants such as privet, forsythia, myrtle, and Norway maples are all that remain. The house, barns, and possibly a greenhouse were all destroyed by fire in the 1940s.

The Yellow Trail continues through a small grassy field and back to the "T" intersection, where a left turn will return you to the Orange Trail. Turn right on it and go back the way you came.

15. Arthur W. Butler Memorial Sanctuary

Location: Mt. Kisco, New York
Distance: 3 miles
Access: From I-684 take Exit 4, Mt. Kisco. Go north on NY
172 (toward Mt. Kisco) 0.25 mile. Turn left on Chestnut
Ridge Road. Follow this road 1.2 miles to the entrance on
the right. Parking.
Owner: The Nature Conservancy

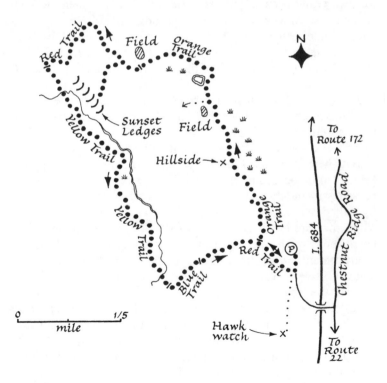

RIDGES AND RAVINES, HUGE GLACIAL BOULDERS,

a field with wood lilies, a cattail marsh, and a small pond where birds come to drink and bathe — all await you at Butler Sanctuary. There is a special area complete with bleachers, high above I-684, that is a noted hawk-watching place during fall migration.

Walk from the parking area, past the entrance sign, along the Red Trail. Look for the Orange Trail and turn right. In a small overgrown field to the left of the path, a large pinxter azalea blooms in May. Thick carpets of haircap moss border the trail. Most of the other shrubs here are highbush blueberry.

The Orange Trail continues into a deciduous woodland with very little understory. A huge ash beside the trail has an unusual shape. Perhaps the weight of a dead tree once lay against this branch. By the time the dead tree decayed, the branch was permanently deformed. Other peculiar shapes in trees are caused when the leader, or foremost-growing tip of a tree, is broken. Side branches then alter their directions of growth in an effort to replace the leader, resulting in interesting convolutions of the tree's trunk. This is especially noticeable in some of the tulip trees along this trail. Tulip is a very soft wood, easily broken in storms.

The Orange Trail runs at the base of a hill rising on the left, with a swamp on the right. There is a mix of ferns along the way. Where the trail enters a small field, turn right, still on the Orange Trail. In a short distance you approach a small pond. There is always bird activity here. Most birds like to bathe. Feathers are fragile and must be kept in good condition. In addition, birds are host to various parasites including feather lice, mites, and a hideous-looking flat fly called a hipoboscid. Humans only encounter these creatures when they are handling birds, as they do during banding. Fortunately none of them are parasitic on mammals. Some birds, such as grouse and pheasants, will dust bathe to rid themselves of their fellow travelers. You may see these dust-bathing places in open areas of the trail.

Past the pond, the Orange Trail turns left, paralleling a cattail marsh behind the pond. There are several poison sumac shrubs on the edge of this marsh and many clumps of red maples. Sensitive fern grows to enormous size here. As the trail approaches a large field, there are some interesting tulip trees on the left.

This meadow is ever changing. Indigo buntings sing from the

tops of the red cedars in spring, when the whorled loostrife is in bloom. In late June wood lilies raise their orange cups along the side of the path that edges the left side of the field. Goldenrods and stiff asters bloom in September, when grasshoppers and crickets are in chorus. Near the end of this section of the trail are several clumps of bayberry.

Wood Lily

From the field, turn right on the Red Trail. Shortly there is another trail to the left. This side trail dead ends on Sunset Ledge. It is a lovely place to sit and eat your lunch, with nice views to the west any time of day. A clump of one of the more unusual milkweeds, four-leaved milkweed, blooms here in May.

Go back to the Red Trail and turn left. In many places throughout the sanctuary you may see pieces of orange tape on trees. A study of flying squirrels has been going on at Butler for some years. These tapes mark areas where the squirrels den, and there may even be an occasional live trap in view. Please do not disturb them. Through monitoring the squirrels' activities with radio collars, much information is being garnered. It has been discovered that female squirrels set up and defend territories against other females. They frequently change denning sites during the raising of their young, probably leaving nests that are infested with fleas for cleaner surroundings. The squirrel population varies directly with the production of acorns. Occasionally the resident naturalist at Butler conducts night walks to look at these beautiful little rodents.

At the junction with the Yellow Trail, turn left. Here you enter an area with many fascinating boulders strewn about. They are good denning areas for raccoons and foxes. You can make a good guess as to who lives where by looking for scats, the droppings of wild animals. Raccoon scats often contain seeds from grape and bittersweet. Skunk scats may be made up almost entirely of the exoskeletons of beetles and yellow jackets. Fox scats, usually formed of fur with bits of broken bones, have a twist at the end. The droppings of deer look like black jellybeans. This kind of observation may offend some people, but it is often the best way to find out what animals are sharing a woodland with you.

Many of the large rocks in the ravine you now enter have beautiful growths of polypody fern on them. The soil which supports this lush growth is very thin and can be peeled away from the rock like a rug. Damp and cool, this area includes a little brook which runs near the trail. At the Blue Trail, turn left. The trail rises to the top of a ridge, where it intersects the Red Trail once again. Bear right on the Red Trail and walk through fragrant groves of white pine and Norway spruce back to your car.

16. Westmoreland Sanctuary

Location: Mt. Kisco, New York

Distance: 2.5 miles

Access: From I-684 take Exit 4, Mt. Kisco. Go north on NY 172 (toward Mt. Kisco) 0.25 mile. Turn left on Chestnut Ridge Road. Follow this road 1.3 miles to the sanctuary entrance and parking area on the left.

Owner: Westmoreland Sanctuary, Inc.

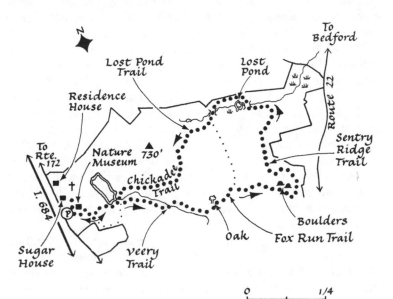

WESTMORELAND'S HANDSOME MUSEUM WAS originally a church, built in 1782. In 1950 the church was dismantled and stored in a barn. Much of the material in the museum, which was reconstructed in 1973, is from the church. Hand-hewn beams support the interior. The exhibit cases, made from barn siding, are in keeping with the architecture. They contain examples of local fauna from fish to deer, as well as interesting artifacts found on sanctuary land. The sanctuary encompasses 625 acres and has much to explore.

Start your walk on the Easy Loop Trail, to the right of the building. This will bring you to Bechtel Lake. Standing on poles in the water at the far end of the lake are two kinds of bird houses. The tall metal cylinders are intended for wood ducks. While the metal may be hotter than wood, it protects the ducks from predation by raccoons, which cannot climb metal. The houses' location cannot alone protect the birds, since raccoons are good swimmers.

The smaller, wooden boxes are occupied by tree swallows. These handsome birds, with bluish backs and white bellies, swoop constantly over the water catching insects on the wing. Their nests are made of grasses and many feathers. White feathers from other birds are highly favored, and the birds must sometimes fly long distances to find them. The young swallows differ from other songbirds in that they can fly well at the time they leave the nest. Birds such as robins spend their first few nest-free days on the ground. Were fledglings from nests over the water to flutter out into the water, they would not survive (except, of course, for ducks). The young swallows may not feed themselves efficiently for a few days, but the parent birds continue to provide.

Take the next right turn. There is a large patch of red trillium at the base of the trail sign. Now turn left in a few steps onto the Veery Trail. All the trails in this sanctuary are marked by yellow plastic squares on the trees, but the intersection signs will guide you. The Veery Trail parallels the outlet brook from the lake. Some of the trail goes through an evergreen forest. One of the smaller of these evergreens is red spruce. In its preferred mountain home, red spruce is an important lumber tree. Here in the lowlands it is rather scrubby. You can recognize the red spruce by a gall that grows on its twigs. Galls are insect-caused swellings on plants. They are plant specific — the aphids that cause this swelling on the red spruce live on no other plant. New galls are green; old unoccupied ones are brown and covered with minute holes where the aphids have emerged.

In sunny spots along the brook, look for water striders. Their shadows are easier to see than the insects themselves. Each of their legs makes a dimple in the water surface. If you watch the shadows, you can see how the striders "swim" on the water: the middle pair of legs propels the bug, the hind pair steer, and the front pair are held up in readiness to capture another insect as food. The bugs must stay in motion here to keep from being washed downstream.

Turn left on Fox Run Trail. This part of the forest is open, with very tall trees and patches of sunlight. In some of these patches bracken fern grows. Another name for this fern is eagle claw, because as it unfurls it looks like a large bird's claw. Its spores are held under the leaflets' rolled edges. In the shadier parts of the trail there are large stands of bugbane, holding its white candles of flowers aloft in late June. Like many members of the buttercup family, bugbane flowers have no petals. The flowers are clusters of stamens that have a fluffy appearance.

As you go up a short hill look on the left for a large, dead white oak with five trunks. Just beyond this tree is a patch of shinleaf. Its waxy white drooping flowers have a sweet smell that is worth getting on your knees for. They, too, bloom in late June and early July. The leaves of the plant are evergreen.

Turn right on Sentry Ridge Trail. Keep a sharp lookout for one of the most uncommon ferns of the area, rattlesnake fern. Its feathery triangular leaves have a fertile stalk rising from their apex. This fern grows singly, rather than in clumps.

At one point on the left of the trail are some unusually large, very white quartz boulders. The trail tops out along the edge of a high ridge. You can almost see down the chimney of a house below. In May listen for the ringing call of the hooded warbler. This handsome little bird, with its bright yellow face and black hood, nests close to the ground but sings its song high in the trees.

Now the trail makes a long descent to the edge of Lost Pond. There you will find a nice bench on which you can sit to observe the antics of the dragonflies in July. One of the large ones, the white-tailed dragonfly, patrols a territory over the pond. Each male has a favorite perch to which he returns. From it he will chase any other male that flies nearby. The females have brown bodies and are welcomed into the males' territories.

Follow the trail around the pond and turn right, still on the Lost Pond Trail. At the next intersection turn left on Chickadee Trail. Here you are close to the base of some of the more spectacular rock formations in the sanctuary. Columbine, ferns, and grasses grow from crevices. There are small intriguing caves, and the convolutions of the rocks are very beautiful.

The Chickadee Trail will return you to the end of Bechtel Lake. Walk up the hill and take the second right turn to get back to the museum.

17. Ramsey Hunt Sanctuary

Location: Cross River, New York

Distance: 2.5 miles

Access: From I-684 exit at NY 35, marked "Cross River/Ka-
tonah." Go east (toward Cross River) 1.9 miles. Turn left
onto North Salem Road. Continue 0.8 mile to a small parking area on the road's left side, before you come to the sanctuary's sign.

Owner: National Audubon Society
(Managed by Bedford Audubon Society)

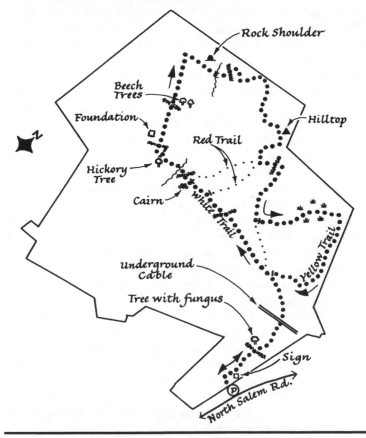

ALMOST ENTIRELY WOODED, RAMSEY HUNT Sanctuary contains a great variety of trees, including beech groves and oak-hickory woods. The sanctuary also offers an interesting swamp walk, with numerous little bridges and a rather ingenious way of using small sticks and brush to cross some of the damper places.

Follow the White Trail, which starts at the parking area's back right corner. Because neighborhood horses are ridden on these trails, they may be a bit chopped up in places. The trail goes first through a young forest mostly made up of sugar maples. Vines climbing up these trees, including grape, poison ivy, and woodbine, offer good fall food for migrating birds. Large flocks of robins and rusty blackbirds frequent this cafeteria in mid-October.

As the trail passes through a stone wall, a large old tree on the left bears several artist's fungi. These woody shelves have that name because their white undersides retain any marks made upon them, whether fingerprints or real drawings.

The only open area in this sanctuary is the telephone underground cable corridor. This provides the "edge" so well liked by birds and small mammals. Continue on the White Trail. You will pass an intersection with the Yellow Trail. Where the White Trail divides, take the left fork. The woodland here is shrouded with bittersweet. This vine, imported from the Far East many years ago, is an aggressive climber and will kill many of these trees by strangulation. Our American bittersweet, uncommon in the lower part of New York state, is not so aggressive. You can tell the two apart because the Oriental vine has clusters of berries in each leaf axil, whereas the American has berries at the ends of branches. Before fire in the forest was so rigidly controlled, these vines would probably have been kept in check by occasional fire outbreaks.

In a short distance you will pass both ends of the Red Trail. There is a wide, very wet stretch of trail here which is used by horses, and the white markings bear to the right to keep your feet dry. Small bridges rise over a stream, where green frogs sit on mosses and rocks. The trail goes through a wall, with a large hickory tree in attendance, and turns sharply to the right. On the left, beyond another stone wall, is an old foundation. The size of some of the stones in old walls and foundations is impressive when you think that they were moved by men and oxen or horses, not by modern mechanized monsters.

This section of the White Trail passes through a beautiful beech forest. From the light green of unfolding leaves in spring, through to their glowing yellows and browns in the fall, beeches seem to exude sunlight. The trail makes another sharp right and descends to a stream with a bridge. Off to the left you can glimpse a massive shoulder of rock. Beechdrops, the parasite of beech tree roots, are abundant here. Another fascinating plant that has no chlorophyll grows near the far end of the bridge — pinesap. This plant is not a parasite but a saprophyte which takes its nourishment from decaying material in the soil. In late summer the pinesap comes up a pale yellow color; in October the stems bearing its ripening seeds are rose-pink.

Beyond the bridge you will climb a steep slope. In the summer months Ramsey Hunt is well populated with a special spider called a Micrathena, which likes to build its orb webs directly across paths. In such a wooded area the clearing provided by this path may be a sort of flyway for insects. Sometimes the anchor lines of these orb webs are ten or more feet long, going out to surrounding vegetation. The Micrathena spiders themselves (there are several species) have spiny, hard, shiny abdomens that are triangular in shape. As they hang in the middle of the webs, the spiders appear top-heavy. They are harmless, so should you walk into a web you will only suffer a faintly unpleasant sensation of webbing on your skin. (Try not to be your group's leader!)

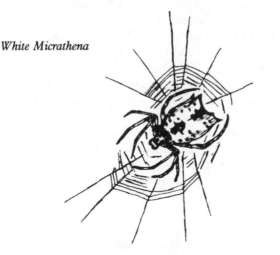

White Micrathena

At the top of the hill the path bears left to a rocky overlook. Masses of May apple bloom here in the spring. As the trail descends again, look for deer tongue grasses along the right side. These grasses have very wide blades that turn yellow and brown in the fall.

At a "T" intersection, turn left, still on the White Trail. About 50 feet beyond an opening in a wall, the White Trail makes a sharp right. The apparent trail to the left goes to a private house, as do several others around the edges of this sanctuary. Should you make an error, you will soon discover it and have to turn around. The White Trail now leads over another rock outcropping, where you may put up a ruffed grouse. Walk down a long slope and at the bottom turn left onto the Yellow Trail.

The Yellow Trail winds through a nice swamp. Near the trail's start is a large bed of mixed ground pine and ground cedar, two of the lycopodiums. In the fall their spores are ripe. Shake one and see the yellow clouds come out. These spores are highly explosive. Before the days of electric bulbs they were used to make flash powder for cameras. Cinnamon ferns are also abundant here. In spring their spore-bearing stalks, separate from the leaf fronds, are the color of cinnamon. In fall the fronds turn cinnamon as well. Our deciduous holly, the winterberry or Christmas berry, is common in swampy areas, with bright red fruits which hang on far into winter. It is thought that some of these fruits only become palatable to birds after they have been frozen.

As you leave the swamp the trail makes a short (perhaps 10 feet) jog to the left, then turns sharply right up the hill. An old fallen tree demonstrates what foresters call the "pillow and cradle" effect. The tree's uprooted base makes the pillow, and the hole makes the cradle.

The Yellow Trail takes you through good deer habitat and once more back to the White Trail. If you are suddenly startled by a loud snort, that is the warning a deer gives so other deer in the area will be aware of human intrusion. Deer are not known to attack people, even during rutting season when the bucks' tempers are short. But the loud snort is scary to hear.

Turn left on the White Trail. It will lead you back to the parking area.

18. Marian Yarrow Nature Preserve

Location: Cross River, New York

Distance: 1 mile

Access: From I-684 exit at NY 35, "Cross River/Katonah."
Go east (toward Cross River) for 2 miles. Turn left onto Mt.
Holly Road. At 0.2 mile bear right at a "Y." Continue 1.2
miles to a 90° left-hand turn. Drive 0.8 mile to the sanctuary
sign. A small parking area is on the right.

Owner: The Nature Conservancy

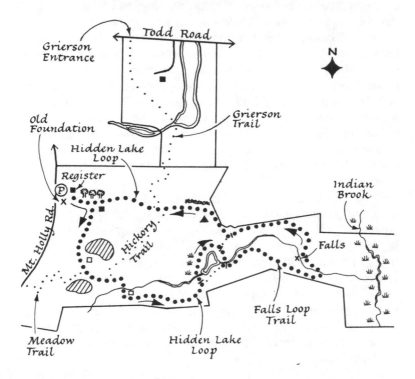

THE NATURE CONSERVANCY MAINTAINS SEV-
eral sanctuaries in the Cross River area. While they are not large,
they provide refuges for mammals and birds that thrive in woodlands
rather than in suburban surroundings. Fine specimen trees, a lake,
and a pretty waterfall await you in the Marian Yarrow Preserve.

Walk from the parking area straight ahead on a wide trail. Maps
can be picked up at a shelter a short way in. Notice the huge sugar
maples on the left. Large trees standing in a younger woodland
evoke memories of former farms, as do the many stone walls mean-
dering through this area. Most of the young trees surrounding these
giants are their offspring. Sugar maple seedlings can grow in the
shade, waiting for a chance to replace their elders. Very few ground
cover plants grow in this dense shade.

Turn right at the Hidden Lake Loop sign. Then continue straight
at a sign bearing the adage, "Let no one say, and to your shame,
that all was beauty here before you came."

The trail crosses a small meadow. Here are several large red cedar
trees, good places to look for cedar waxwings during the fall. Waxwings are very fond of the trees' small blue cones. In summer many
grasshoppers live in this field. Grasshoppers hatch as nymphs from
eggs laid in the soil. Each time they molt their exoskeletons, their
wing pads grow a little. By the time late summer arrives, they are
flying. The males "sing" during daylight hours, some species by
rubbing their hind legs together and some by rubbing their legs
against their wing covers. Grasshopper ears are located on the abdo-
men.

Cross the meadow and continue on the Hidden Lake Loop. Eastern wood peewees can be heard singing far into the summer, their
plaintive "pee-o-wee" coming from the treetops. Since these birds
are flycatchers they like to sit on dead branches high in the trees,
flying out and back on their forages after insects.

Two more small signs direct you to the lake. In any woodland
where black birch is an important component, small pieces of rotting
wood that are turquoise blue in color can be found on the ground.
These are pieces of black birch containing a fungus called
Chlorosplenium. Occasionally you will see its fruiting bodies, which
look like little cups.

Turn left on Bass Trail. A small marsh surrounds an inlet stream
to the lake. In spring the skunk cabbage here is stiff and glossy.

By August it is bent, browning, and full of holes where slugs have enjoyed an evening meal. This trail parallels the lakeshore. You will find small clumps of monkey flower along the lake's edge. Yellow markings on the lower lip of the lavender flower may resemble a monkey face.

Turn right at the end of the Bass Trail. In summer floating duckweed on the lake is pushed by breezes into ribbons and swirls of varying shades of green. In the open water the reflected trees look like part of a tapestry. Near the overflow culvert, swamp milkweed blooms in July. You may see orange and black aphids on its stems. Almost all insects that feed on any kind of milkweed have this coloration. It is a warning to birds that the insects are bad tasting because they have ingested the glycosides that milkweeds contain. Pickerel frogs, with large squarish spots on their backs, hunt insects in the damp grass. They make prodigious leaps to reach the water. Along the shoreline green frogs bask, giving loud squeaks as they jump from under your feet.

Just past the culvert, turn sharply left onto the Falls Loop Trail. This trail descends along the stream through the cool woodland. Visitors can see white-tailed deer on almost any visit to this sanctuary. In summer when their antlers are growing, bucks often hang out together in small groups. The velvet-covered antlers are delicate and sensitive. In order not to bump them on brush or low branches, the buck will lift his head when he runs from intruders, laying the antlers back along his neck.

Where the trail crosses the stream, look to the left for a waterfall tumbling down over a series of rock outcroppings. Its beauty varies according to the amount of water. In spring clumps of hepatica bloom among the rocks alongside the waterfall. In summer there is a clump of pointed-leaved tick trefoil. "Trefoil" refers to the three-part pattern of these plant's leaves, and "tick" refers to the sandpaper-covered seed which sticks to anything that brushes against it.

At the end of the Falls Loop Trail, turn right. Bear left onto the Hidden Lake Loop Trail, paralleling a stone wall. Stay on the wider trail. An orange trail turning to the right leads to the adjacent Grierson Preserve. Should you wish to explore it, on a one-way trail in and back out, be aware that there is said to be quicksand near the Grierson lake and stay on the trail. If you do not choose this option, the wide trail you are on will lead you back to your car.

19. Ward Pound Ridge Reservation

Location: Cross River, New York

Distance: 2 miles

Access: From Interstate 684 take the Cross River/Katonah exit. Go east on NY 35 for 4 miles to NY 121. Turn right and drive 0.1 mile to the reservation entrance road on the left. Minimal parking fee.

Owner: County of Westchester

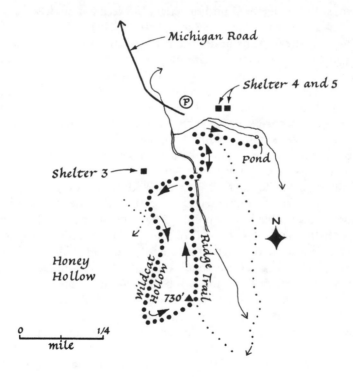

WHEN YOU VISIT WARD POUND RIDGE RESERVA-
tion, be sure to look for bluebirds. They are always in the park,
frequenting the large maples along road edges and near fields. Every
year more than one hundred species of birds are sighted on the
many trails of this large (almost five thousand acres) reservation.

Enter the park and drive up Michigan Road, which is the first
right after the toll booth. Leave your car in the parking area at the
end of the road, and walk straight ahead on the dirt path, bearing
to the right at a fork.

Swampy land on either side of this path sports many varieties of
moss. Mosses, like ferns and fungi, reproduce by means of spores.
The spore-bearing stalks vary in color from bright green to red or
brown. Each capsule has a cover to protect its spores until the
weather is just right for dispersal. Usually the capsule has a hinged
cover, with tiny teeth around the edge. Flowering moss feels to the
hand like an old-fashioned butch haircut.

Where a stream runs under the path, skunk cabbage and marsh
marigolds are abundant. Skunk cabbage is our earliest wildflower
and can actually melt its way up through the last ice and snow. The
color of the protective hood around the spathe of flowers is reminis-
cent of decayed meat, causing pollination by attracting flies and
beetles that normally go to such a source of food rather than to
flowers. In late summer skunk cabbage fruit may be found lying
in the mud, looking like wrinkled brown oranges. Each contains
many beanlike seeds, relished by mice and chipmunks.

Bear right at the next "Y," on the Red Trail. Several hundred
feet along, take an unmarked trail bearing left, which starts just
before you see a big rock shoulder coming up on the Red Trail and
goes off through a thick stand of laurel. (At the time of writing,
this trail was unmarked, but it is officially named the Yellow Trail.)
Flower buds of laurel are small and flat. You can judge during
winter walks where flowering will be best in May. This thick stand
makes a good hiding place for animals. It would be pretty hard for
us to penetrate it — but the deer manage to get in.

We are now approaching Wildcat Hollow itself, a deep ravine
bordered by rocks and hemlocks. Is it possible there are really
wildcats here? These animals are secretive, and none have been
seen recently.

Just at the beginning of a downhill portion there is a flat area
where you can walk, to the right, to a nice overlook above the

swamp that fills this end of Wildcat Hollow. In spring you can look down on frogs chorusing their love songs in the cool sunlight. Last year's hemlock cones are crunchy underfoot. Piles of deer scat indicate that deer, as well as people, like an overlook.

Back to the trail, which is now marked occasionally with yellow paint. It continues on the left-hand side of the stream, but you can meander back and forth according to the depth of the water. Two easily identified mosses are abundant along the way: pincushion, which is pale green-white; and fern moss, yellow-green and looking like a miniature fern. The pincushion is very thick and fairly dry, much favored by small animals for nesting material.

Approaching a rock field and some downed trees, the trail divides. Keep to the left along the ravine floor. You will walk through a large stand of maidenhair fern, very evident with its fan shape and wiry black stems. This is our only large fern with black stems, and it is fairly rare. Its habitat requirements are precise: rich loamy soil and lots of moisture.

Because of Wildcat Hollow's constant moisture, it is a good place to look for woodland salamanders under rotten logs. Two of our area's salamanders are unusual in that they do not have to lay their eggs in water. The red-backed and slimy salamanders place their eggs under logs or rocks, and the developing creatures complete the tadpole stage within their eggs, emerging as tiny salamanders. These animals are very fragile. If you pick them up by their tails the tails may come off, so handle the salamanders carefully and return them quickly to their moist homes.

Where you can obviously go no farther in the ravine because of deadfalls, bear to the left up a hill. Look for a standing dead tree on the left. Its wide furrows are left by a boring beetle larva, obviously one of the larger beetles. Like termites, beetle larvae are able to consume and digest hard wood because of protozoa in their intestines which make it possible for them to gain nutrients from the wood. They are vital links in the forest's recycling chain.

At the intersection with a larger trail, turn left onto the Green Trail. This trail is rather rough going in spots, because it is well used by neighborhood horsemen. After a long descent through mixed hardwood forest, you will come to the Red Trail again. Turn right, and walk back to where Michigan Road is visible. Turn onto the other fork here (the one not taken before) for a short distance, and go across a grassy path to the left. The marsh that stretches between this path and the shelter on the hillside is covered with blueberry bushes. Their red twigs, white flowers, and blue fruit make them decorative at all times of year, as well as a delicious food source for humans and other animals. This marsh has many interesting plants including, in early summer, the beautiful Calopogon orchid.

The path you are on leads to the edge of a hidden pond. This pond was dug for a swimming hole in the 1930s by the Civilian Conservation Corps, which also built the original museum and the camping shelters in this park. Surrounded now by shrubs, the pond is a nice little haven for wildlife, from fish to dragonflies and wood ducks.

On the way back to your car, remember to look for the bluebirds. To visit the park museum, drive back down Michigan Road and turn to the right. A nice combination of old and new, the museum not only houses materials on the wildlife and early times of the area, but also has the finest library of Delaware Indian information in existence. You can pick up a calendar of county park events there, too, and a map of Ward Pound Ridge Reservation, which has many other trails to explore. Several nice ones are a walk along the river from The Meadow Parking Area to Kimberley Bridge, a hike up the Fire Tower Trail, or a longer walk to the Leatherman's Cave.

20. Halle Ravine

Location: Pound Ridge, New York

Distance: 1.3 miles

Access: From the center of Pound Ridge go north on NY 137, and then bear north on NY 124. The first right after Hiram Halle Library is Trinity Pass Road. Go down this road 0.7 mile and park on the edge of the road next to a white gate in a stone wall.

Owner: The Nature Conservancy

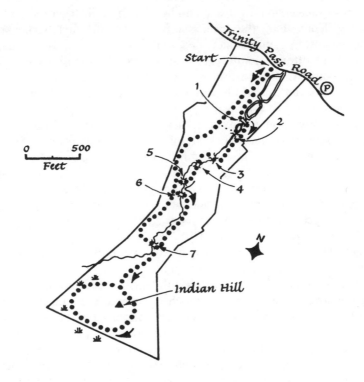

THIS WALK, WHICH PARALLELS A STREAM AND takes you over a series of bridges, lies mostly in the depths of a ravine. Tall trees rise overhead, and visitors sometimes speak of the place's "intimate" quality — an unusual word to use about a natural area.

Go over the stone steps next to the gate, and take your first left-hand path. You will descend on a trail bordered with barberry bushes and cork-bark euonymus, landscaping plants that have been widely distributed in our woodlands by birds. When a bird eats a berry, it digests the soft material and passes the seed through its digestive system, effectively planting the seed along with its excrement.

Two lovely small ponds provide reflections of trees and the sound of frogs conversing with one another. In the fall, leaves sail like tiny galleons along the water's surface. Near the first bridge we find one of the ravine's many decaying logs. The damp breeze that comes up through its deep cleft smells like decaying leaves and mushrooms; many mushrooms are evident. Slugs, squirrels, and chipmunks can eat wild mushrooms without harm, while one bite may prove fatal to a human.

Look upward at the extreme height of these trees. They must reach extra far to get their share of sunlight. Most of the trees in this early part of the ravine are hemlock, beech, and black birch. Climb the stairs beyond this first bridge and bear right. The stairs that continue on your left go to private land. Note the ground cover of partridge berry, green throughout the year. Its twin white flowers, which appear in late June, are followed by a single red berry with two "eyes." A stone bench invites you to sit and look down the length of the ravine. This is only one of several pleasant meditation spots in this sanctuary.

Large flocks of crows are often in the ravine, feeding and bathing in the stream. Crows have a much more highly organized social structure than most birds. A feeding flock usually has a lookout posted to warn the others about humans or other potential danger. Long maligned as the farmer's foe, the crow has been vindicated to a large degree by research which shows the bird eats a great deal of animal matter such as grubs, other insects, and mice. Crows are now protected under federal laws, though states may set hunting seasons for them. In suburban areas the crow is a valuable scavenger of the many animals destroyed by our cars. However, because crows make incredible noises — caws, grindings, garglings, and strangling sounds — large winter roosts are never popular with local residents.

Near our second stream crossing are some nettles. (This is actually bridge number three on your map; we do not cross number two.) You can see the nettles' stinging hairs with the naked eye, but your hand lens, carefully used, will show you the mechanism by which they work: each hair is attached to its stem by a small bulb, and when you brush against the stem the bulb and hair operate like a tiny hypodermic needle. The stinging can last for some time.

Beyond the fifth bridge a large stand of blue cohosh begins. This is a fairly uncommon wildflower, with blue-green leaves and small star-shaped flowers. In fall the plant bears bright blue berries which are highly poisonous. Not even birds eat them. Fine new stonework protects the edge of the stream against erosion, proving that the talent for laying dry stone walls did not die with the builders of our reservoirs.

After bridge six you come up to an open sunny patch with lots of scouring rushes growing. The tissues of these strange prehistoric-looking plants, with green stems and no leaves, contain a great deal of silica. You can feel it if you rub them with your fingers. They were named "scouring rush" because colonial housewives used them to clean pots and pans. The feathery field horsetail is related to this plant.

Do not cross the seventh bridge yet, but continue to the end of the ravine and up over a short stone ledge into a field. You are now on property belonging to the town of Pound Ridge. This field has some exceptional wildflowers in it, most especially fringed gentians in September and October. The beautiful fringed gentian is a biennial; it is a rosette of leaves the first year, it flowers and sets seed the second year, then it dies. There are very few places left in which it can grow, since it favors wet meadows and most of those have gone under the developer's bulldozer.

Climb a very steep hill on the other side of the field. This area is known as Indian Hill. In May you may see another rare flower, yellow lady's slipper, in bloom on the hillside. As the path crosses the top of the hill, look for shells of white-lipped snails. This large (one-inch shell) land snail is a delicacy for birds and mammals. I have found a number of shells with their central whorls chipped away and their tenants eaten. Like all snails and slugs, the white-lipped is a hermaphrodite. Each snail has both male and female sexual parts, but it must exchange genes with a partner to lay fertile eggs. The shell forms within the egg, and a newly hatched white-lipped snail is about the size of a pinhead. These snails feed on decaying vegetation.

The path goes over the top of the hill and down the other side to the edge of a marsh. Turn to the right and parallel the marsh, walking back to the field and back into the ravine. Turn left and cross the seventh bridge, then turn right to bear north along the stream. The trail back is sometimes different from the one you came on and sometimes the same, but when it is the same trail is looks different because you are approaching from the opposite direction.

Reaching again the stonework near the fifth bridge, turn left up some steps by a leaning tree. At the top of the steps turn right. Now you are high above the ravine, closer to the tops of some of the tall trees you passed earlier. Two more inviting benches are set along this trail, where you can sit and watch the activities of birds and other animals below. This ridge trail leads back to the road and your car.

21. Cranberry Lake Park

Location: Harrison, New York

Distance: 1.25 miles

Access: Exit NY 22 at Orchard Street 0.8 mile north of the
Kensico Dam or 2 miles south of the intersection of NY 22
and NY 120. Entrance sign is on Orchard Street, 100 feet
from NY 22. Parking.

Owner: County of Westchester

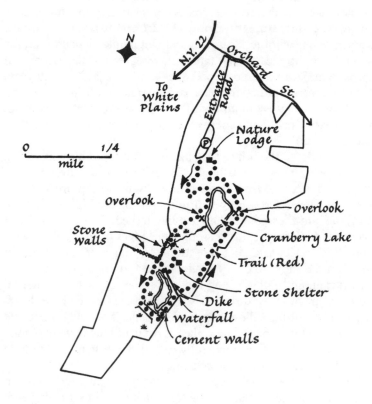

THE BUILDING OF THE KENSICO DAM HAD A
tremendous impact on the Cranberry Lake area. The entire village
of Kensico was destroyed by the filling of Kensico reservoir, and
an influx of foreign workers with their families turned the little
country village of Valhalla into a bustling center. Besides its natural
wonders, Cranberry Lake Park is interesting for its relics from that
time.

From the parking area near the Nature Lodge, take the service
road through the woods toward the lake. Although trap rock on the
road helps to halt erosion, it is noisy and awkward under foot.

The many oak trees of the park drop acorns on the ground, and
in good years walking the Cranberry Lake trails is like walking on
marbles. White oaks bear acorns every year; red and black oaks
take two years to mature their fruit. This acorn crop is very important
to much of our wildlife. Squirrels and chipmunks depend on it for
winter food supplies. Deer fatten themselves for the winter on
acorns. Acorns are eaten by wood ducks and blue jays, too; in years
of sparse acorn production, blue jays migrate south in large numbers. When the gypsy moth population peaks every 10 years or so,
the oaks expend so much energy putting out two sets of leaves they
cannot set fruit.

Turn left down the hill to the edge of Cranberry Lake. In spring
and fall look for ospreys fishing. These large hawks often migrate
over inland lakes. After it dives into the water to capture a fish in
its strong talons, the osprey will not immediately kill its prey. Instead, the bird flies holding the fish in a torpedo-like position until
it is dead. A principal shrub around the edges of the lake is sweet
pepperbush. It is said that the strong fragrance of this shrub in
bloom on the shore told early sailors they were nearing land.

Turn right and follow along the lake shore. In early summer an
interesting plant called downy false foxglove can be seen here. Nota-
ble for its beautiful yellow flowers, the plant is actually a parasite
on the roots of oak trees. The spikes of brilliant blue flowers blooming in shallow water are pickerel weed. Pickerel may like to hide
among this plant's underwater stems.

Bear right up a short steep hill. At the top is an overlook from
which you can see the lake, some of which is swiftly turning into
a marsh. Hummocks with sedges, ferns, blueberry bushes, and red
(or swamp) maple saplings are abundant. The rare calopogon orchid
glows pinkly on the hummocks in July.

A fascinating insect called a pelucid wasp can often be seen in these woods, flying low among the shrubs. These wasps are predators on wood-boring beetle larvae. They have very long — two- to three-inch — ovipositors trailing out behind them. Ovipositors are egg-laying appendages which look like gigantic stingers but are actually used for drilling into dead wood and finding beetle larvae. An egg is laid which will hatch into a wasp larva; it will feed on the larva of the beetle.

Few natural cataracts, such as this one at Cranberry Lake Park, exist in Westchester.

Turn left on the dirt road, and observe the stone wall along the right-hand side, dry-laid and perfectly aligned. Many of Westchester's beautiful stone walls were built by skillful masons brought to this country from Italy, Ireland, and Scotland to build our great dams, the Croton and the Kensico.

Turn left again, past (in May) clumps of pink lady's slipper orchids, onto a short bridge over the stream. This is a good place to look for bird activity over the lake and for sunning water snakes near the stream (the snakes are harmless — we don't have water moccasins in New York). The path from the end of the bridge leads you to a park mystery. The stone structure along the trail may have been built for a farm house root cellar (that a house was here seems evident from the abundance of day lilies), a hideaway for slaves during the underground railway period, or a storage place for the Kensico dam workers.

This path leads to a dike separating the park's two ponds. The dike was part of a transportation system for granite quarried from private land to the east of the park and carried by train to the dam construction site on the other side of NY 22. The old pilings in this upper pond were part of a trestle for the train. The Kensico dam is unusual in that is was finished several years ahead of schedule. It's worth visiting after your walk, just a short way south on NY 22. An area called the Dam Plaza is also a county park. In Kensico Lake are mixed waters from all members of the great Catskill and Adirondack aqueduct system.

At the upper pond, which is shallower than Cranberry Lake, painted turtles can usually be seen sunning themselves on logs. "Painted" turtles are so called because their heads have yellow stripes and their shells have red and yellow stripes along the edges. They are one of our most common local turtles, favoring shallow ponds. As they lie in the sun they are digesting their food of water plants and small water animals. The heat of the sun is necessary for digestion, since they have no internal heat of their own.

Turn right on the dike, then left on a path that leads along the edge of the upper pond to another bridge. From it the arching stems of a lavender-flowered plant called water willow can be seen over the hummocks. In the water near the end of the bridge is some bladderwort, an interesting little plant with yellow flowers in July. It uses the bladders on its underwater stems to siphon in small animals, which the plant then digests.

90

Turn left at the end of the bridge. Cement walls on the right are the foundation remnants of rock crushers and loaders used to place quarry stone onto train cars.

By the next intersection is a lovely waterfall. Turn right up the hill through laurel to an overlook from which you can see the lake spread before you. Bear left again along a trail that parallels the Cranberry Lake shore. This fairly wet and brushy area is excellent for birding, especially during spring migration. Back at the Nature Lodge you will find exhibits of local flora and fauna, with a naturalist in attendance Wednesdays through Sundays all year.

22. Marshlands Conservancy

Location: Rye, New York
Distance: 1.5 miles
Access: From I-684 take NY 287 east to Exit 11, Rye. Go right
  (south) on US 1 for 2.6 miles. The conservancy entrance
  sign is on the left, just past the Rye Golf Club. Parking.
Owner: County of Westchester

THE MARSHLANDS CONSERVANCY MAY BE THE jewel of the county park system. Its great variety of habitat — woodland, field, and seashore — provides something of interest at every season. Marshlands also has a small museum with exhibits of local flora and fauna, including saltwater aquariums in which you can see some of the sea creatures up close.

Beginning behind the museum, the trail goes first through a grove of crab apple trees. The colors of their blossoms and, later, of their fruit are various and beautiful. These trees provide fruit long into the winter for birds and mammals. As we enter the woodland, we are surrounded by sweet gum trees. The sweet gum, with its star-shaped leaves and spiky fruit, is normally found in wet areas farther to the south. Here is an almost pure stand of this handsome tree.

Along the trail on the left, a huge tree trunk lies on the ground. Because this land was once a private estate (the John Jay homestead), it supports many exotic plants. This tree was a sweet or mazzard cherry, one of the biggest ever seen. By looking at its standing stump you can tell that the tree has been riddled by carpenter ants, which chew galleries in the wood. They do not actually ingest the wood, so there are piles of sawdust on the ground under the fallen trunk, an indication of ongoing ant tunneling. When wood is infested with termites there is no sawdust. Termites are able to digest wood because of bacteria that live in their intestines. Ants feed on other insects and use the tree as a home.

The Woodland Trail leads us to the edge of a large field. At one time this was a wheat field; then it became a small airfield. Since World War II it has been allowed to grow naturally, except for annual mowing. In July the field is a mass of orange butterfly weed; in September its goldenrod, sunflowers, and purple asters are spectacular.

Following along the edge of the field, we are walking on a small plant that looks like a grass but is actually path rush. Since the rush does not grow very high, it is not mowed. Walking on it actually improves the chances of its seeds reaching the ground, so they can sprout. The presence of this rush in a place where many feet pass by helps to prevent erosion of the trail.

Bear to the left as you approach the bend at the end of the field, and walk out to an overlook above the marsh. Spread before you is a vast harvest of marsh grasses. As winter storms mat down and tear at the marsh grasses, they become the basis for a thick, delicious soup which is the beginning of the food chain for millions of organisms living here. In turn, these tiny zooplankton become food for fingerling fish that spend their early lives in such protected areas. Crabs, mussels, clams, snails, and many other creatures live and feed in the marsh. If the tide is low, the exposed mud flats may be covered with fiddler crabs. These small animals live in holes in the mud. The males have one much-enlarged claw, which they wave enticingly in the face of the females, and which they also use to fight off other males.

This is one of the best places anywhere to see snowy and great egrets, great blue herons, and the night herons — both black- and yellow-crowned. At low tide the birds feed on marsh animals; at high tide they roost in the trees on small islands near the marsh's edge.

Coming back onto the trail from the overlook, bear to the left and follow the path downhill between dense thickets of catbrier. Now you are at the level of the marsh, walking on a low dike with the marsh on your left and a bay on your right. A beautiful tall grass here is called switch grass. Marsh mallow blooms along the dike edges in June. Its soft gray-green leaves are velvety. Originally, marshmallows were made from the roots of this plant. The dike goes out to Marie's Neck, which you can circle in either direction. Be very careful of the poison ivy. It grows in this sandy location like a three-foot hedge.

At last you reach the seashore itself, with beautiful rock outcroppings of mica schist glittering in the sun. Along the beach or caught up in the grasses you may see cast-off shells of horseshoe crabs, those ungainly monsters of the seas which have remained unchanged in form and function for millions of years. In late May and early June horseshoe crabs come to this beach during nighttime high tides to mate and lay their minute blue eggs.

The deeper waters of Milton Harbor host ducks of many kinds, along with herring, great black-backed, and ring-billed gulls. Occasionally a population explosion of starfish provides fun and games for these birds. You may see an oyster dredge taking up small oysters, which will be transplanted to cleaner waters to complete their growth. Shellfish from these waters are not fit for human consumption. Cormorants swim in the harbor, sometimes with just their heads and necks showing snakelike above the water, or they may sit on pilings drying their wings.

Each composite "flower" is actually a bunch of flowers, with disc florets in the center and ray florets as "petals."

Tides bring in a lot of human garbage. This park's naturalist never goes anywhere without a garbage bag and sees to it that this shoreline is one of the cleanest anywhere. (She will be glad to give you a bag, if you would like to help.)

Retracing our steps to the edge of the field, we can choose to walk back through a different woodland path or along the edge of the field itself. Pheasants may fly squawking away, or an osprey may circle overhead. Great horned owls nest in the sanctuary, probably feeding on rabbits from this field. A last small bridge leading into the woodland toward the museum is guarded by a beautiful English oak. Along this bit of trail we can also see European sycamore, or plane trees, and turkey oaks, whose acorn cups are decorated with long bristles.

FAIRFIELD COUNTY

Collis P. Huntington State Park

23. Audubon Center in Greenwich

Location: Greenwich, Connecticut
Distance: 1.5 miles
Access: From I-684 exit at NY 22, Armonk. Go north on NY
22 to a stoplight. Turn right onto NY 433. Continue 2.5
miles to the center (on the left). Parking.
Owner: National Audubon Society

THE AUDUBON CENTER, WHICH HAS A GREAT
variety of habitats for visitors to enjoy and a wonderful shop, also
offers an interpretive section with exhibits, an observation window
by the bird feeders, and a teachers' resource area. Its summer
Ecology Camp for adults is well known.

From the parking lot, walk down the paved road and turn left
through the orchard on the Interpretive Trail. These old apple trees
attract many birds. Bird houses around the edge of the orchard are
used by bluebirds, tree swallows, and house wrens. Look on the
trunks of the trees for rows of little holes made by the yellow-bellied
sapsucker, a woodpecker that specializes in drinking sap and eating
small insects attracted to the sap.

This trail bears right into the woodland, past a small vernal
(springtime) pond, and down to the edge of Lake Mead. Turn left
at the bottom of the hill. Almost immediately there is a short dead-
end trail on your right which goes out to the edge of the lake. Look
closely in the mats of sphagnum moss along the edge of this muddy
trail for sundews, small carnivorous plants which are very uncommon in our area. One sundew's rosette of round leaves can be
entirely hidden by a silver dollar. The leaves are covered with hairs
and drops of a sticky fluid which attracts insects. A hapless insect
will stick to a leaf as the plant slowly folds the leaf over and ingests
the insect's body. Carnivorous plants grow in wet, acid areas. Some
of the nutrients necessary for their growth are obtained from their
victims.

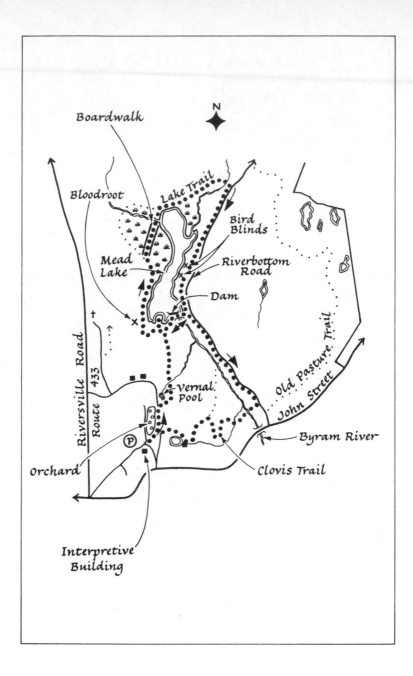

Go back to the trail and turn right. Where the trail turns right once more, there is a huge patch of bloodroot. Its white flowers appear in early April, when the plants' leaves are folded around their stems. After the flower petals have dropped, the leaves unfold and continue to expand. The seeds of the bloodroot bear an unusual appendage common to most seeds of the poppy family. It is a white, succulent-looking protuberance called a caruncle, and its function for the seed is debated. Some people believe it absorbs moisture, increasing the seed's chance of sprouting. Others think that it is attractive to ants, and that the ants, in removing the caruncle, scratch the seed coat and thus improve the seed's ability to sprout.

At the next intersection, turn right onto the boardwalk. Ferns grow junglelike on the hummocks in the water. One of the shrubs that can be seen here, poison sumac, is rarely observed from dry land. Growing only in wet places, poison sumac's compound leaves have no teeth and are not as numerous as those of the staghorn and other red-fruited sumacs. Its leaflets are egg shaped, with a long pointed tip. Poison sumac develops white berries which hang like little bunches of grapes, very much like the berries of poison ivy. Also like poison ivy, this sumac can cause dermatitis in humans, so look but don't touch. In fall the shrub turns a marvelous shade of orange, blazing away in its watery oasis.

Dragonflies zoom in to land on the boardwalk's handrails. These beautiful insects spend several years of their lives in the water as nymphs. When they are ready to become adults they crawl onto the land, cling to a rock or plant stem, split down the back, and come out with wings. Adults and nymphs both feed on other insects.

Look down into the pools for small frogs still retaining some of their tadpole tails. For most species, this amazing transformation takes place in July. The dramatic caterpillar-to-butterfly metamorphosis takes place in the pupa, while the insect is not visibly active. But in the case of tadpole-to-frog, the whole configuration of the animal changes while it is still swimming about. The mouth changes, lungs take the place of gills, even the intestinal system changes from the long, involved system of a plant eater to the shorter one of an insect eater. Stored food in the tail is absorbed during the last stages of this change.

Some of the exposed rocks or plant roots here are good places for basking water snakes, which are aggressive if they are picked

Old apple trees are some of nature's most beautiful sculptures.

up. Their tiny teeth can make pinholes in your skin, but no harm will come of it, since the snakes are not venomous. One of their usual activities is eating those little frogs. But then, small water snakes are often readily eaten by bullfrogs, which will snap at anything that moves, including others of their own kind.

Other animals that may swim right under your feet include spotted turtles and snapping turtles. Spotted turtles are becoming very scarce. The same cannot be said for snappers. I saw a huge one here, with a head the size of a human fist.

At the end of the boardwalk, turn right. Cross the stream that feeds into the lake, and continue to take each right-hand fork to follow along the lake shore. Stop at the first bird blind. You can sit quietly here, observing the activity among hummocks and shrubs in the water. Perhaps a wood duck will swim quickly by. A phoebe builds a nest inside this blind, so leave the panels over the observation slits open.

Continue along the lake to the dam. This is a fairly high dam, and you can walk on the top of it to enjoy the water thundering over and splashing up as it hits the V-shaped rock below. There are liverworts on the rocks near the edge of the dam. Examined with a hand lens, liverworts look like reptilian skin. They are ancient plants, somewhere between mosses and ferns in development, with similar reproductive cycles.

Come back off the dam and continue down the wide trail paralleling the Byram River. Cross over on the second bridge, and continue on the Clovis Trail. You will come to a small pond close to the cluster of buildings and then back to the place the walk began.

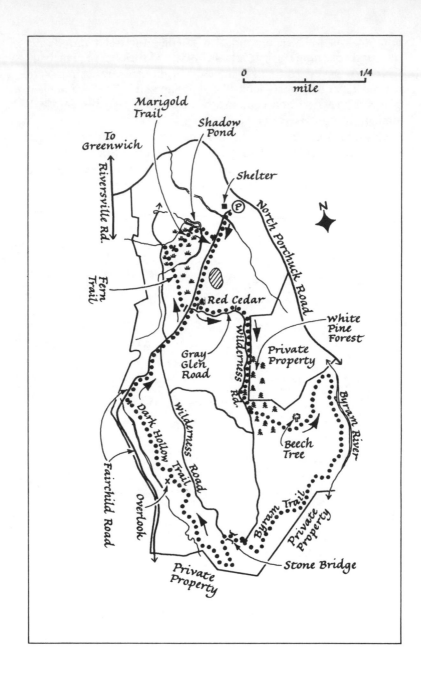

24. Fairchild Wildflower Garden

Location: Greenwich, Connecticut

Distance: 2.3 miles

Access: Exit I-684 at NY 22, Armonk. Go north to a stoplight and turn right onto NY 433. Continue 4.4 miles to North Porchuck Road (the second left after the Audubon Center in Greenwich). Follow this road 0.5 mile to the entrance on the right, identified by its green gates. Park inside the gates.

Owner: National Audubon Society

ORIGINALLY DEVELOPED AS A SPECIAL PLACE for wildflowers, Fairchild Garden also offers a trail next to a river, a spectacular gorge, wet meadows, and a pond. From your car walk along Fairchild Road, past the shelter. In front of the wall through which Beech Trail passes is a large patch of galax, with round, leathery leaves. This plant usually grows farther south. On the right is a pond which can be scanned for herons and turtles.

Continue on Fairchild Road. Shortly you will come to a small meadow ringed with bayberry and maleberry bushes. The bayberry leaves have a wonderful smell. This is not the bay used in cooking. The berries, waxy and gray, are used to make bayberry candles. Maleberry looks very much like blueberry, but instead of berries, its fruits are dry brown capsules.

Turn left at a very large red cedar, onto Gray Glen Road. Because red cedar is a pioneer tree, usually growing in old fields and soon shaded out by black birch and maple, it is remarkable to see so many large red cedars in these woods. The bark may be shredded by squirrels. It makes good nesting material, perhaps even helping to keep down fleas and other vermin, just as the wood of red cedar keeps moths out of human clothes.

Listen for the crowing of a cock pheasant. These handsome birds were imported from China to England and then to North America. They seem comfortable living close to human beings. Ground nesting birds are very susceptible to nest destruction by foxes, raccoons, and dogs — one reason unleashed dogs are unwelcome in wildlife sanctuaries.

Turn right on Wilderness Road. This pine forest is home to little red squirrels, smaller and more aggressive than gray squirrels. Piles of pine cone scales under the trees show where they have been feeding. In addition to the chatter of squirrels, the forest offers the sound of wind high in the trees and the fragrance of needles underfoot.

Turn left onto the Byram Trail. As you descend through the pines you will enter a grove of beech trees. Scattered at their bases are plants of the beechdrop, a parasite on the roots of beech trees. The beechdrop has no chlorophyll. It is red and white when first in bloom, drying to brown. Apparently it does no harm to the roots on which it grows. An abundant wildflower along this trail is wild sarsaparilla, with two compound leaves on a woody trunk. On a separate stalk from the leaves is an umbel of greenish flowers in May, followed by blue berries in midsummer. Roots of this plant used to be an ingredient in root beer.

The Byram River, originating in many small swamps and ponds, achieves a good width and flow here. It contains many beautiful rocks, little rapids, and pools. Very early in the spring you will see stoneflies on the rocks and on tree trunks along the river. Stonefly nymphs live in such cold rushing waters. The adults survive a very short time, just long enough to reproduce. These insects are a favorite food of trout.

Byram Trail bends away from the river and goes up a long slope with many dead trees on the ground. Such fallen wood provides a good medium for a variety of mushrooms. Reaching Wilderness Road once more, turn to the left. Cross a stone bridge and take a trail on your left which turns steeply downhill. This is Dark Hollow Trail. At the bottom of the hill, the trail turns to the right. Then the trail rises along the rim of a deep gorge sparkling with mica schist, one of the basic rocks of the area. At the very top of this hill is a nice overlook where you can rest and watch waterfalls coming down the other side of the gorge. Beside the overlook is a large witch hazel bush, another native plant formerly used for medicinal purposes and now largely replaced by chemicals. Witch hazel

Ice forms first around rocks and along slow-running edges of the Byram River.

is the last of our shrubs to flower. In October it is covered with yellow flowers which have threadlike petals. At the same time the fruits from the previous year are maturing. As these fruits ripen, their inner membranes shrink. Finally with a loud pop the outer covering bursts, and hard black seeds are thrown several feet from the parent plant.

At the end of the Dark Hollow Trail turn right onto Fairchild Road once again. Then turn left onto Fern Trail. This will lead you into the wet meadow. In spring many blue flags and large patches of May apple bloom here. In late summer the field is ablaze with goldenrod, with the pink-and-white flowers of arrow-leaved tearthumb sticking up at all angles over the goldenrod. If you wonder why it is called tearthumb, run your fingers lightly up a stem. Large clumps of purple ironweed and the reddening leaves of the white fruited, gray-stemmed dogwood shrub add more color. At the end of the Fern Trail is a bench where you can sit and be scolded by catbirds in the shrubbery. Turn right on the Iris Trail, then left on the Marigold Trail, which will bring you to the side of the pond and then back to Fairchild Road near the parking area.

25. Bartlett Arboretum

Location: Stamford, Connecticut

Distance: 0.75 mile

Access: From the Merrit Parkway take Exit 35 onto CT 137 North (High Ridge Road). Continue 1.5 miles, passing the Stamford Museum and Nature Center, and turn left onto Brookdale Road. Follow Brookdale to the arboretum entrance. Parking.

Owner: State of Connecticut

Caution: Do not take this walk if conditions underfoot are wet. Algae on the arboretum boardwalk can be dangerously slippery.

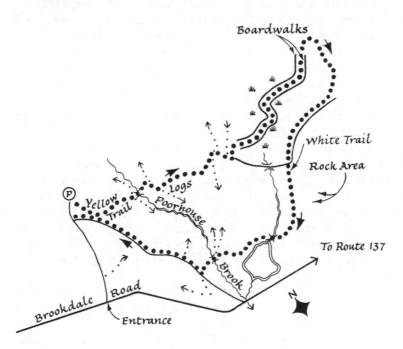

THE BARTLETT ARBORETUM OFFERS A COMBI-
nation of natural and man-controlled environments. Its various specialty plantings — nut trees, dwarf conifers, azaleas, and rhododendrons — are of great interest to the home landscaper and amateur botanist. The greenhouse, which is cared for by volunteers, is one of the most interesting I have ever seen. Ask in the office if you may visit it.

To enter the natural woodland and boardwalk area, take the Yellow Trail from the parking lot. You will walk through a typical New England woodland of oak, hickory, and beech. On the left of the trail is a dramatic cathedral-like cluster of beech growing on top of a rock. One of the trees is dead and is full of interesting holes which look like good spots for raccoons or owls.

Cross the bridge over Poorhouse Brook and look along the trail for some very large specimens of Solomon's plume, or false Solomon's seal. This plant is so called because each year when the flowering stem dies back, a round depression which looks like a seal is left on the rhizome, its underground stem. These rhizomes are not buried very deeply. A little scraping away of the soil will show you the "seal." True Solomon's seal, whose flowers and fruits hang from each leaf axil (rather than from the end of the leaf stalk as in the "false"), grows here too.

Turn right and then left where there are a lot of large rotting logs on the ground. These logs are important to the small animal life of the forest. In summer they are daytime hiding places for millipedes, sow bugs, and centipedes, as well as red-backed salamanders. If you like to pick up such creatures for closer examination, watch out for the centipedes. These flat, reddish animals are predators on insects and other small animals. They can bite rather hard, and they have a poison in that bite which will make your finger sting for several hours. Because centipedes are predatory they are very fast moving, unlike the rounded, brown millipedes which only feed on decaying plants.

In winter, logs like these are hibernating places for animals such as the white-faced hornet queen. Its queen is the only member of the hornet community to survive the winter. In early spring she emerges from her hibernating log and starts to build a paper nest. As she lays eggs and raises workers, the nest slowly grows. When there are enough workers to supply the colony with food and building material, the queen stays in the nest and continues to lay eggs. She is fed by the workers. These hornets feed on other insects. The

110

paper nest may grow to the size of a football, or even larger. When cold weather comes all the inhabitants of the nest except the queen will die. The nest is never used a second time. It is often torn apart by woodpeckers seeking larvae and pupae that may remain in it at the end of the season.

Along the trail past the logs, large masses of wood anemone bloom in April. Near the intersection, turn briefly left and then right. You are approaching a wonderful boardwalk which runs at a height of several feet through a swamp. However, the red pine of this boardwalk does grow algae. If the boards feel at all slippery when you step on them, please stay off.

One of the major plants in this swamp is arrow arum, a relative of skunk cabbage and jack-in-the-pulpit. Its flowers, on a stalk called a spadix, are hidden inside a long green spathe. As the seeds ripen, the stem holding them bends gracefully down into the mud, planting the seeds in their preferred habitat. Other beautiful swamp plants to be seen are silky dogwood with white flowers or blue berries, large clusters of royal and sensitive fern, and winterberry — a deciduous holly with inconspicuous flowers but blazing red fruit. In late summer the cardinal flower contributes its bright red flower stalks to the scene.

At the end of the boardwalk, turn right. In late summer the edges of this woodland trail will be covered with white woodland aster. Evergreen plants such as spotted wintergreen and partridge berry are here, too. Where the wide woodland road turns right, continue straight ahead on the White Trail. You have to negotiate your way through what looks like a glacial dump. Rocks of all sizes are everywhere, many of them with beautiful growths of mosses and lichens. In April dwarf ginseng nestles among the rocks. This trail crosses a bridge over the inlet to a pond.

Continue on the trail along the edge of the pond, and turn right on a service road. In spring this hillside is an extravanganza of daffodils. The road will bring you back to the entrance road, from which you may explore the arboretum's many specialty gardens.

You might like to combine your visit to Bartlett with a visit to the Stamford Museum and Nature Center, where you can see captive wildlife such as white-tailed deer, owls, raccoons, and skunks. The museum usually has an art show along with other exhibits. There is a planetarium, as well. The parking fee at the museum is $5 for non-Stamford residents.

26. New Canaan Nature Center

Location: New Canaan, Connecticut
Distance: 1 mile
Access: From the Merritt Parkway take Exit 37. Go north on
 CT 124 for 2.8 miles. The center is on the left side of CT 124
 (Oenoke Ridge), 0.5 mile north of town. Parking.
Owner: New Canaan Nature Center Association

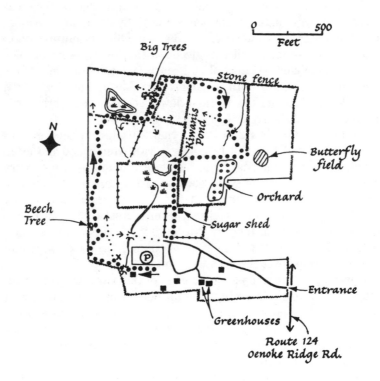

THERE IS SO MUCH GOING ON AT THE NEW
Canaan Nature Center, it is difficult to decide whether to walk first
or to begin by exploring the center's exhibits and the horticultural
building. The later, with a contemporary passive solar design, is
full of delightful plants. When you do start to walk, take the path
on the left edge of the parking lot. As you enter the woodland,
there is a huge patch of stinging nettles on your right, with all its
nasty needles glistening in the sun.

Fruit for birds is evident on holly and viburnum bushes on the
right, as well as on a large poison ivy vine clambering up a tree on
the left. As you follow the trail, bearing slightly to the left, there
is an unusually large mockernut tree on your left. This tree, of the
hickory family, has a nut that is almost as good as the shagbark's,
with a thinner husk. Nuts such as these are eagerly sought by
squirrels and chipmunks for winter stores. The animals remove the
husks before burying or storing nuts, for husks absorb water and
cause decay of the nuts inside. Empty husks found on the ground
in winter usually have small grubs eating away inside them.

Gray-green lichens decorate the bark of the mockernut tree.
Lichens do no damage to the substrate on which they grow. They
are a combination of an alga and a fungus, living in a symbiotic
relationship. The fungus secretes an acid to help in holding on, and
the green alga makes food which they both consume. Because lichens
are very sensitive to air pollution, their presence in such abundance
indicates that the air of this region is fairly good.

Listen and look for chipmunks as you walk. When close by, the
chipmunk's scolding sounds much like a little squirrel's. Sometimes
you may hear an apparently distant sound like two sticks being
struck together. This is another chipmunk warning noise, which
has a ventriloquial quality. I have seen chipmunks doing it, and
they puff out their cheeks, keeping their mouths closed. These little
ground squirrels are not true hibernators. They do retire underground during the winter and sleep for long periods of time. However, along their tunnels are store rooms full of nuts, berries, and
seeds. Should a chipmunk awake during cold weather, it has a nice
supply of food. Other rooms in the long tunnel system are used for
nesting areas and bathrooms. Wild animals do not soil their own
nests.

Bear right (the left trail through the stone wall goes to private
property) and then slightly to the left. This sanctuary has many

large trees. Along this trail on the left is a beech with some carving on it. Probably the first graffiti was carving on trees and scratching on rocks. Much as we deplore the practice now, it is sometimes interesting to read signs others have left. The earliest date I can find on this tree is 1946.

As is true of all former estate lands, New Canaan Nature Center has many exotic shrubs, such as forsythia and euonymus. A very large, partially hollow, native white ash is on the left of the trail. Continue straight ahead, under a mulberry tree. Because mulberries are many birds' favorite food, these trees are often planted in orchards to keep birds away from other fruits which ripen at the same time, such as cherries. The purplish berries can be very messy underfoot, however, so if you plant a mulberry tree to attract birds to your yard, don't put it where people walk.

Bear right toward the pond. If you approach slowly, you may see a muskrat swimming or foraging along the pond's edge. Muskrats are rodents which have adapted, like beavers, to life in the water. Their fur is soft and waterproof. Sometimes they build small lodges, beaverlike in design but made of reeds rather than sticks. More frequently they tunnel into banks or the water side of dams, which does not endear them to human pond keepers. Muskrats have naked scaly tails, flattened from side to side, which they use as rudders.

Go through the stone wall and turn left onto an old farm road. On your left, just before the next intersection, are two gigantic trees

Cup Plant

in an open area. One is a swamp white oak, the other a red maple. Both have girths that should make them candidates for a "Big Tree" register somewhere.

Turn right, then right again, and then left. This trail leads into an open field which the nature center calls a "butterfly field." The area is mowed to keep it from reverting to forest. At one end is an orchard. Apple cider making is one of the fall events here. The trail makes a hairpin turn, and on the right is a large stand of cup plant, one of the more unusual of the plants that resemble sunflowers. Its large leaves grow around its stem, making a cup which retains rain water. The trail leads to the edge of the Kiwanis pond. Many local organizations contribute to the New Canaan Nature Center. The outlet from the pond makes a nice marshy area, with cattails and other wet ground plants providing shelter for nesting birds. On the way back to the main buildings you might visit the maple syrup shed, which is active in earliest spring when the sap begins to rise.

27. Seth Low Pierrepont State Park

Location: Ridgefield, Connecticut
Distance: 3 miles
Access: From Ridgefield take CT 35 north to CT 116, turn left, and follow CT 116 for 2 miles. Turn right onto Barlow Mountain Road. At the first intersection turn left, still on Barlow Mountain Road (straight ahead becomes North Street). The Pierrepont entrance is on the right between two white posts. Parking.
Owner: State of Connecticut

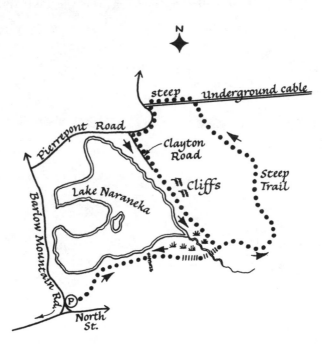

PLEASANT VIEWS ACROSS NARANEKA LAKE, specimen trees, and a steep trail to a high ridge with unusual vegetation are among the attractions of Pierrepont State Park.

On the left of the parking area is a large patch of May apple. The one-inch white flowers hide between pairs of umbrella leaves. They are followed in late spring by yellow egg-shaped fruits, reputedly edible but of questionable taste. Mandrake root is another name for this wildflower. In the middle of the parking area is a very large honey locust tree. The clumps of thorns on its trunk look vicious. It is from this tree that many of the thornless, fruitless, domesticated forms of the locust have been developed.

Mayapple

Follow the White Trail from the parking area. Huge sugar maples grow near the trail, their ancient trunks pocked with hollows where branches have fallen and decay has taken place. These make ideal homes for raccoons, flying squirrels, and even honeybees. In spring ginger, bloodroot, and doll's eyes bloom here. Later in the season blue lobelia enjoys the damp soil.

Where the trail goes through a stone wall, there is a small forest of scouring rush. The trail, rather worn, has many exposed roots. In several places there are short spurs which lead to the edge of the lake. Mute swans, beautiful European additions to our bird population, nest on the lake in spring. The adults can be seen with their gray cygnets from late spring until ice up.

In the marshy area where the stream enters the lake, broad-leaved arrowhead blooms in summer. Known also as duck potato, this plant's roots are favored food for ducks during fall migration. Wild mint and mad-dog skullcap are two other flowers which grow in

117

Connecticut residents can get permits to launch boats for fishing on Lake Naraneka.

the marsh. The skullcups are named for the shape of their seed receptacles.

Logs have been placed in the wettest places to aid your passage. At the end of this corduroy bridge, the trail turns right. You will see evidence of pileated woodpeckers in this area. The ground is liberally sprinkled with large chips in many places. Listen for the loud clucking of this crow-sized woodpecker.

118

Most of the trees at this lower elevation are red and sugar maples, tulip trees, and ash. The trail begins to wind upward and at one point is very steep. Now laurel appears, with red and chestnut oaks. There are a number of striped maples, with green-striped bark when young and large leaves in the shape of a goose's foot. Hop hornbeam also appears, its bark finely shaggy. Hornbeams were once used to make yokes for oxen. Both these trees prefer high elevations and are much more common farther north than in this area.

When this land was farmland there were probably nice views from this ridge over the lake. Now trees mask the lake in summer. The trail reaches an open area which has been cleared for an underground telephone cable. Here is a chance to see some of the flowers that prefer meadow situations, such as goldenrod. Turn left and follow the clearing steeply downhill until it meets Pierrepont Road. Turn left on the road, then left again on Clayton Drive.

Along the left side of the road are tall plants of figwort. The flowers are not spectacular, shiny green outside and brown inside, and they are best appreciated with a hand lens. This plant is in the snapdragon family. The figwort blooms in late May and June. Later in the summer soapwort, or bouncing Bet, can also be found along this road. Soapwort was used in colonial times to make suds for washing clothes. It is still employed to gently clean old fabrics and tapestries.

At the end of Clayton Drive the trail enters the woods once more, near the edge of the lake. Beech is the predominant tree here. Rock cliffs of impressive height border the trail on the left. When you come to the intersection with the log crossing on your right, turn right and follow this trail again, back to your car.

28. Devil's Den

Location: Weston, Connecticut

Distance: 2 miles

Access: From the Merritt Parkway, take Exit 42. Go north on
   CT 57 for 5 miles. Turn right on Godfrey Road. Go 0.5
   mile and turn left on Pent Road. This road dead ends in the
   preserve's parking lot.

Owner: The Nature Conservancy

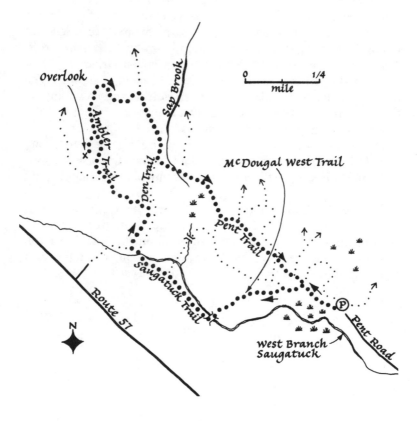

DEVIL'S DEN IS SO NAMED BECAUSE SOME OF ITS
rocks bear hoofprint marks. Turn-of-the-century charcoal makers
said the marks had been burned in by the Devil's hot feet. This
large preserve has so many interesting trails, you will want to return
many times. Permits are required, but one can be obtained on your
first visit without charge.

Take Pent Trail at the parking lot's far left corner. Each trail
intersection is marked by a large post with a number. At Post 3,
bear left on McDougal Trail. Then bear left again at Post 17. This
is the Saugatuck Trail.

One of the abundant plants along the way is hog peanut. This
fragile trailing vine has small white or pale lavender flowers which
form pods, each with several seeds. These seeds are not edible.
However the plant also has a single flower at the base of its stem
which develops a single seed below the ground's surface, as peanuts
do. This seed is edible but not especially delicious, according to
the edible food books.

Two very successful practices at Devil's Den prevent your slipping
on log crossings over streams. They are topping such logs with
chicken wire, or scoring them with a saw. You can still retain your
footing even if the logs are wet.

After you descend some log steps, look along the left of the trail
at about 20 feet for a patch of rattlesnake plantain. This is an orchid
with mottled evergreen leaves in a rosette. The flowers are borne
on a six-to-eight inch spike in late June. They are so small you will
need a hand lens to appreciate their form.

Cross the west branch of the Saugatuck River on a wooden bridge.
The water is very brown, probably from high tannin content. It is
also very clear and inviting.

There are many dead hemlocks along this trail. Oak trees can
withstand several defoliations by gypsy moths, providing other conditions, such as adequate rainfall, are good. Evergreens cannot
recover if they are defoliated even once. Under these trees there is
a mat of dewberry, a blackberry that crawls along the ground. In
June black-wing damselflies flutter weakly from perch to perch.
When they are young these beautiful insects live in the water of
streams and rivers. The male has a bright turquoise body, while
the female has a black body and a white wing spot.

Do not turn right at Post 13, but continue a short distance to the
next, unmarked, right turn. Turn left at Post 12. On a log at the

121

base of some rocks look for powderhorn lichen. There are three kinds of lichen: crustose, foliose, and fruticose. The first hugs the substrate closely. The second, such as the rock tripe which you will see a lot of in this preserve, may be attached at only one point. Fruticose lichens have upright spore-bearing stalks, as in this powderhorn or in British soldiers.

Only the passage of an occasional plane mars the feeling of remote wilderness of Devil's Den.

Bear right at Post 46. Here the right side of the trail is bordered by laurel, while the left side is solid with sweet pepperbush. The trail itself seems to divide well-drained soil, which the laurel prefers, from very damp soil where the sweet pepperbush grows. At Post 45, turn left to walk out onto an overlook. There are many pink lady's slipper orchids nestled under the laurel bushes. This orchid blooms in mid-May, to be followed by laurel in late May and early June.

Go back to Post 45 and bear left. In July you can nibble your way along through lowbush blueberries. Huckleberry is here, too, its fruits ripening a little later.

The pines on this exposed rocky ridge are pitch pines, with three needles in each cluster. A large patch of moss on the left of the trail has reindeer lichen mixed in and clumps of Indian pipe in summer.

It is necessary to insert a warning here: copperhead snakes inhabit this ridge. Copperheads are beautiful coppery-brown in color, with darker brown milkbone shapes across their backs, solid color heads, and bright pink tongues. They are venomous but not as dangerous or as aggressive as rattlesnakes. One crawled past me, about three feet away, and slid into a crevice where I saw two more. Just watch where you put your hands and feet.

The trail now descends into a beautiful gorge, with a stream rushing along through rocks. Another uncommon plant which is found in several places along these lower trails is Indian cucumber root. Its flowering stalk stands above a whorl of leaves. Three blossoms are dependent below three more leaves. They hang down in order to be readily available to their pollinators, bumblebees, which cruise close to the ground looking for flowers. After the flowers are pollinated their stalks straighten up above the top leaves, and dark blue berries form. The name indicates that the root of this plant is edible. Perhaps that is one reason it is not common.

Turn right at Post 44, then left at Post 10. This brings you back to Pent Trail and straight back to the parking lot. Other Devil's Den trails have interesting things such as an exhibit to show how charcoal was once made. This was a widespread and dangerous occupation in the 1800s. There is also an abandoned sawmill site, with a monstrous machine which was called "portable." The preserve's director can tell you where to look for the devil's footprints.

29. Putnam Memorial State Park

Location: Redding, Connecticut

Distance: 1 mile

Access: From the Merritt Parkway take Exit 45, CT 58 (Black Rock Turnpike). Follow CT 58 for 13.8 miles to its intersection with CT 107. Bear left at the triangle and enter the park at the statue of Israel Putnam. Park along the road inside the park.

Owner: State of Connecticut

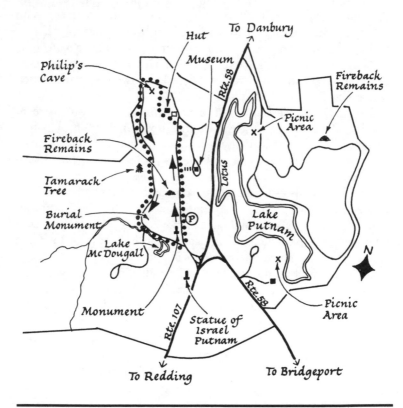

ONE OF THE OLDEST STATE PARKS IN CONNECTI-
cut, Putnam is maintained as a memorial to an encampment of
Revolutionary War soldiers under the leadership of General Israel
Putnam during the winter of 1778–1779. The statue of the general
was made by Anna Hyatt Huntington when she was in her nineties.
It shows him, during one of his escapes from the British, riding
his horse down steps cut into a cliff. (Other sculptures by this noted
artist can be seen at the nearby Huntington State Park — Walk
30.) While this park is not considered primarily a "nature" park,
there is much for a nature lover to see here.

Leave your car anywhere along the dirt road. The first thing you
will notice are piles of stones along the left of the road. These stones
are the remnants of chimneys and fireplaces from wooden huts that
sheltered the soldiers. Each fourteen by sixteen-foot hut held from
eight to twelve soldiers. When they lived here, the entire area must
have been barren of trees, for all wood was needed to keep warm
and make cooking fires. Now the slopes are clothed with the typical
oaks, hickories, and ashes of this climate. On the right you will see
stairs to a nice museum, where you can pick up a map explaining
what each of 11 numbered posts commemorates.

Where a sign on your right directs you to a roadway entrance to
the museum, turn left on a dirt path. Here is an entire chimney
from a hut. In the puddles along this path pickerel frogs jump
before you, disappearing in puffs of mud. The path climbs up to
a hillside of jumbled rocks where caves may have provided some
additional shelter. They are not really caves but more like shallow
rock shelters. Certainly the hill itself would have helped keep the
winter wind from the huts below. A stout railing helps you make
your way along the front of this slope.

There is a lot of jewelweed near the end of this path. Most of it
is the more unusual form, *Impatiens pallida* or yellow jewelweed.
While the rocky path provides a good place to watch migrating
birds in spring, the jewelweed is where you should look for hummingbirds in fall migration. These tiny birds, weighing about two
grams, must eat half their own weight each day in order to fuel
their active bodies. Most of this energy comes from nectar, but
some comes from tiny insects and spiders. During chilly nights or
rainy days hummingbirds go into a state of torpor, during which
their body temperatures and heartbeats slow down. This is the only
way they can survive to another day. They increase their weight by

125

General Putnam's British opponent sent the General a new hat to replace the one with a bullet hole after this escapade.

50 percent before taking off for their long migration, which carries them to Mexico and Central America. The ruby-throated is the only hummingbird in our country's Northeast. Hummingbirds are indigenous to the New World.

At the end of the cave path, turn left on the dirt road once more. Occasional unmarked footpaths branch off, which seem to have

126

been made by revelers and rock climbers and don't go very far. On the right of the road, between two stone parapets, are some young tamarack trees. The tamarack or larch is our only deciduous conifer. Its needles grow in tufts and are of the softest green, turning to gold in late fall before they drop to the ground.

The road continues, with a monument on the left marking the site where fifteen soldiers who died during the encampment are buried. On the right is a small pond with dragonflies and whirligig beetles. Return to your car, drive out of this section of the park, and go left on CT 58. In about ½ mile turn right to enter the other part of Putnam Memorial Park, which surrounds Lake Putnam. The road running through this section has many places to pull off, with picnicking facilities. The lake itself is very beautiful, and has a nice surprise that I have found nowhere else in our area — American lotus. This handsome water plant has large pleated leaves, yellow flowers which look like silk, and big round seedpods, each seed held in a hole in the seedpod's top. Such pods are often used for dried bouquets. Leaf, flower, and seedpod all stand a foot above the surface of the lake. Other plants in the water include white water lilies, blue pickerel weed, and arrow arum.

30. Collis P. Huntington State Park

Location: Redding, Connecticut
Distance: 4 miles
Access: From the Merritt Parkway take Exit 45, CT 58 (Blackrock Turnpike). Follow CT 58 for 10.9 miles. Turn right on Sunset Hill Road. Continue 0.8 mile to the entrance on the right. Drive in and park on the grass.
Owner: State of Connecticut

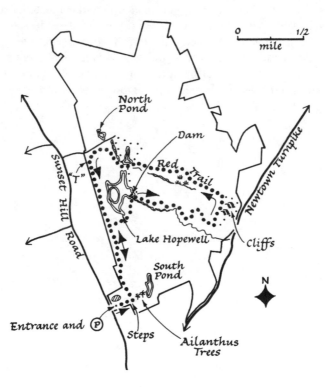

REMOVED FROM MAJOR HIGHWAYS ON A NAR-
row country road, Huntington State Park seems to be known mostly
by people who live in its near vicinity. Wide trails that are well
maintained, beautiful woodlands, fields, and a large lake make it
well worth a visit. The parking area entrance is graced by two
statues sculpted by the noted wildlife artist, Anna Hyatt Huntington,
whose home this was. One depicts a mother bear with cubs and
the other a pair of howling wolves.

On a clear day your first treat is a distant view of eastern Fairfield
County's rolling hills. On the left of the parking area is a large field.
Green in summer with waving grasses, in fall this field is a kaleido-
scope of goldenrod and asters. Take the main path straight ahead,
down the hill next to the field. Along the right edge is a shrub, the
leaves of which resemble black locust. This is not a sapling black
locust, but false indigo. In June it bears spikes of purple flowers
with orange stamens, and in fall it has spires of short brown seedpods. Though the identification book says it does grow in places
like this, in other areas I have only seen it next to rivers and salt
marshes.

After descending some steps you will turn left. Ailanthus trees
rise across from the steps. Both sides of the trail you are now on
are host to many alien species of plants. Bittersweet and multiflora
roses make an impenetrable hedge on either side of the path. In
the fall privet's blue berries emerge here and there from this tangle.
In spring old apple trees still bloom, their trunks pitted with holes
of the yellow-bellied sapsucker.

Turn right at the first intersection. Suddenly the forest is made
up of native trees and herbaceous plants. In spring these oaks are
host to singing yellow-throated vireos. At the edge of this lake in
spring elderberry blooms, its black fruits ripening in September.
On the right at this point is a huge rock, with the roots of a black
birch writhing over it like snakes. Polypody ferns and mosses grow
along the rock's crevices.

Continue on the wide path. Look under laurel bushes along the
left for patches of true wintergreen. The flavor of its leaves reminds
me of teaberry gum. Small white flowers in late spring are followed
by red berries in October. The path emerges onto Lake Hopewell's
dam, with marsh St. Johnswort (the only pink member of its family)
blooming among the rocks in September.

At the end of the dam turn right. This is the Red Trail. It descends through a deciduous woodland, with a brook off to the right. Waves of ferns grow beneath the trees. Ferns can be identified with a bit of study. There is much color variation between them. Most of the ferns here are hay-scented or New York, both a light yellow-green in color and both dying down in the fall after turning rust and brown. Hay-scented fern is covered with a light silver fuzz and has a pleasant odor. New York fern has leaflets tapering at both ends of the frond. Among these are also occasional clumps of cinnamon and interrupted fern. Cinnamon fern bears its spores on a separate stalk in early spring. There is always a tiny tuft of "cotton" at the base of each leaflet, if you look on the back, and the fern's stems are also very fuzzy. Interrupted fern, when it does fruit, bears its spore capsules in the middle of the frond — thus "interrupted." It does not have the cotton tuft or so much fuzz on its stems.

Perhaps the easiest way to learn the ferns is to start with the evergreen ones. Some of these, such as Christmas and marginal shield fern, are very different in color from the herbaceous ferns. Christmas is dark green, and marginal shield almost turquoise. Both have much thicker leaflets than do the hay-scented or New York; this helps them retain water during the hard days of winter.

Turn left, still on the Red Trail. You will be staying on the Red all the way back to the lake. Listen for the crested flycatcher in the spring. On the right tall cliffs rise above the trail. Turn left again. A stream flows downhill to the left of the trail, and an occasional striped maple can be seen. At one point where the stream is close to the trail, a black birch growing on a rock in the stream supports a wrist-thick vine of hairy poison ivy.

Poison ivy is one of our most common plants. It is also a versatile plant. As here, it can be a vine. In sandy soils it can be a shrub. Its leaves turn beautiful colors in the fall, and its small white berries are enjoyed by many birds, including flickers and yellow-rumped warblers, who distribute the seeds from its berries to new areas.

Bear left, still on the Red Trail. When you reach the lake once more, turn right. Looking down the lake from this point you can see a small stone structure which looks like a lighthouse on an island. It dates back to the late 1800s, when the land's owners kept a steam paddlewheeler on this lake. Now that boat is said to be lying under the water.

As you cross a bridge between the main Lake Hopewell and its

130

It is doubtful whether there is enough wilderness left east of the Hudson River to support black bears in the lower states.

East Lagoon, look to your right for a second bridge. It is a nice place to sit and watch natural events. A friend and I sat here one day eating lunch, throwing crumbs to the fish below. We heard splashing around a bend in the cove, and suddenly an osprey flew into view, bearing a large fish in its talons. Since it was late June, this brought us hope that the once-endangered bird might be breeding nearby.

Do not cross this second bridge, but go back and continue on the main trail. In August look across the East Lagoon to see swamp mallow blooming. When the trail reaches a "T" intersection, turn left. Dame's rocket, a member of the mustard family with one-inch, white-to-lavender, fragrant flowers, blooms here from May into the summer. This makes a pleasant garden flower, and I have found that if I cut some at home for a bouquet, side shoots develop and extend the plant's season for bloom. Please do not take any from the park; you can find Dame's rocket along many roadsides.

This wide path traverses the area that must have been used for farm animals when the Huntingtons lived here. Apparently Anna Hyatt Huntington kept horses, cows, and other animals so that she could study them for her statues. On the left, one stone building houses a huge boiler. Another seems to have been a stable, perhaps for cows or pigs. Large sugar maples shade the dirt road. You almost expect to see a horse and carriage come along. This road brings you back to the steps where you will turn right, ascend the slope by the meadow, and return to your car.

Guidebooks from Backcountry Publications

Written for people of all ages and experience, these popular and carefully prepared books feature detailed trail and tour directions, notes on points of interest and natural phenomena, maps and photographs.

WALKS AND RAMBLES SERIES

Walks and Rambles on the Delmarva Peninsula, by Jay Abercrombie $8.95

Walks and Rambles in Westchester (NY) and Fairfield (CT) Counties, by Katherine S. Anderson $7.95

Walks and Rambles in Rhode Island, by Ken Weber $8.95

25 Walks in the Dartmouth-Lake Sunapee Region, by Mary L. Kibling $4.95

BIKING SERIES

25 Bicycle Tours in Maine, by Howard Stone $8.95

25 Bicycle Tours in Vermont, by John Freidin $7.95

25 Bicycle Tours in New Hampshire, by Tom and Susan Heavey $6.95

25 Bicycle Tours in the Finger Lakes, by Mark Roth and Sally Waters $6.95

25 Bicycle Tours in and around New York City, by Dan Carlinsky and David Heim $6.95

25 Bicycle Tours in Eastern Pennsylvania, by Dale Adams and Dale Speicher $6.95

CANOEING SERIES

Canoe Camping Vermont and New Hampshire Rivers, by Roioli Schweiker $6.95

Canoeing Central New York, by William P. Ehling $8.95

Canoeing Massachusetts, Rhode Island and Connecticut, by Ken Weber $7.95

HIKING SERIES

Discover the South Central Adirondacks, by Barbara McMartin $8.95

Discover the Adirondacks 2, by Barbara McMartin $7.95

50 Hikes in the Adirondacks, by Barbara McMartin $9.95

50 Hikes in Central New York, by William P. Ehling $8.95

50 Hikes in the Hudson Valley, by Barbara McMartin and Peter Kick $9.95

50 Hikes in Central Pennsylvania, by Tom Thwaites $9.95

50 Hikes in Eastern Pennsylvania, by Carolyn Hoffman $8.95

50 Hikes in Western Pennsylvania, by Tom Thwaites $8.95

50 Hikes in Maine, by John Gibson $8.95

50 Hikes in the White Mountains, by Daniel Doan $9.95

50 More Hikes in New Hampshire, by Daniel Doan $9.95

50 Hikes in Vermont, 3rd edition, revised by the Green Mountain Club $8.95

50 Hikes in Massachusetts, by John Brady and Brian White $9.95

50 Hikes in Connecticut, by Gerry and Sue Hardy $8.95

50 Hikes in West Virginia, by Anne and Jim McGraw $9.95

The above titles are available at bookstores and at certain sporting goods stores or may be ordered directly from the publisher. For complete descriptions of these and other guides, write: Backcountry Publications, P.O. Box 175, Woodstock, VT 05091.